TWO PATIENTS

Two Patients

My Conversion from Abortion to Life-Affirming Medicine

By John Bruchalski, M.D.

with Elise Daniel

Foreword by Mary Lenaburg

IGNATIUS PRESS   SAN FRANCISCO

Cover photo by Sr. Elizabeth Ann Binder, S.V.
© by Sisters of Life

Cover design by Riz Boncan Marsella

© 2022 by Ignatius Press, San Francisco
All rights reserved
ISBN 978-1-62164-516-0 (PB)
ISBN 978-1-64229-229-9 (eBook)
Library of Congress Control Number 2022934517
Printed in the United States of America ∞

To my wife, Carolyn, and our sons, J.P. and Joseph

CONTENTS

FOREWORD

Everyone's life tells a story, and what you're about to read is a powerful one. I will never forget the first time I met Dr. John Bruchalski. It was my first appointment with a gynecologist in a few years, and my health history was complicated both morally and physically. I knew that Tepeyac OB/GYN was a Catholic, pro-life practice, and I was concerned that I might be judged and treated differently because of my past reproductive choices. I was nervous, but he and his practice came highly recommended by several trusted friends, so I was willing to take a chance.

Dr. B greeted me with kindness and understanding and absolutely zero judgment. He set my mind and heart at ease and answered every question I had, from both a medical and a moral standpoint. Before I left his office, he prayed with me and set me on the path my heart had been seeking. But one of the greatest gifts of that visit was that over the course of the next two decades, he and his beautiful wife, Carolyn, would walk with my husband and me through the most traumatic and difficult time in our lives, leading up to the death of our daughter Courtney.

In September 2014, my 22-year-old profoundly disabled and medically fragile daughter was sent home from the hospital and placed in hospice. After battling a seizure disorder and other ailments for two decades, her body was tired and her liver and kidneys were failing. Knowing nothing about hospice, I called the most compassionate physician I knew. Once again, Dr. B led us through very challenging moral and medical decisions and assisted us in creating a hospice plan that would meet the requirements set by Courtney's care team.

That's what Dr. B is known for: his compassion and empathy in meeting you right where you are and being the face of Christ to you in that moment. His capacity to be present with his patients, no matter who they are, introducing truth and hope into whatever is happening, is legendary. He has a powerful gift for offering gentle encouragement during deliveries and sharing a mother's heartfelt grief when things go wrong.

Through his powerful conversion, Dr. B was able to see the truth about the dignity of the human person. He had intense spiritual experiences that may seem impossible for you or me even to comprehend, but I am reminded often that every life is unique and each of our stories is different. Dr. B's openness to Our Lady's guidance, Our Lord's mercy, and the Holy Spirit's wisdom is what helps him and his staff at Tepeyac remain faithful to the pro-life mission he was divinely given more than three decades ago.

Dr. B's unyielding commitment to protecting life from conception to natural death played a beautiful part in assisting us in choosing rightly for our daughter throughout her life. His obedience to Our Lady was on daily display in how he interacted with everyone, from patients to insurance companies to other physicians who did not always agree with his convictions. These disagreements never swayed Dr. B. He has been willing to undergo intense scrutiny and harassment, even to the point of persecution within his own field of medicine, because he refuses to allow his faith to be lukewarm.

Dr. B's witness to life changed me and my husband. He brought a different perspective to life and death, one for which we are forever grateful. I will never forget that last 48 hours of our daughter's life—Dr. B stopping by the house to check on her, asking how he could pray for us, and bending over Courtney's bed to tell her how grateful he was for her sufferings and sacrifices in these last hours of her life this side of heaven. His presence brought profound peace to me and my family. He was gentle but honest when explaining what death looks like so that we would be prepared for our daughters' final moments on earth.

He was the one we called after she had taken her last breath. He came at two o'clock, smiling from ear to ear. He felt honored that God had chosen December 27, the feast of Saint John the Beloved and his name day, to call Courtney home. He went to her bedside, kissed her forehead, and immediately began to say the Rosary. Then he waited with us patiently as we made all the necessary calls. At the most traumatic and tragic moment of our life, he was there, smiling, praying, offering us hope for a new day. I am incredibly thankful for his guidance and support that day and since then.

Three years later, our relationship changed once again, and he became my boss as I took a job in the front office of Tepeyac. I witnessed pro-life work firsthand, and it was not easy. The challenges the staff faced daily with funding and spiritual warfare were not for the faint of heart. I remember Dr. B said to me once, when asked how he kept the doors open to assist both the insured and uninsured women who came seeking medical care: "Mary, there has not been one day since we opened those doors that someone can say this practice is about me. It's all about Jesus and his Mother, and the work they are doing though each one of us here. Everyone has a part to play in honoring life. No one stands above another. We are a team. Always."

When I left the practice to complete my first book, *Be Brave in the Scared*, and to begin speaking internationally about my story, Dr. B continued to hold my family in prayer, calling especially upon the intercession of our daughter Courtney.

As you, dear reader, dive into the pages of *Two Patients*, be prepared to be challenged, inspired, and encouraged to live out your faith with passion and conviction. Dr. B's story is not just a story of a change of heart, but a story of what happens afterward. He has changed the way pro-life medicine is practiced and has challenged the culture of health care for women. Every person's life tells a story, and his is a story of conversion, redemption, purpose, and mission. I am immensely grateful that my family has been a small part of it. So thank you, Dr. B, for your obedience to God's call. May the Holy Spirit continue to guide you in your mission to bring the truth to women everywhere.

Mary Lenaburg
Author of *Be Brave in the Scared*
and *Be Bold in the Broken*

ACKNOWLEDGMENTS

It takes a small village to write and publish when you are busy delivering babies and seeing patients. Thank you to Chaney Mullins Gooley for initiating the book idea and pushing me through my reluctance to share my conversion story with the world; and to my good friend Will Waldron for believing in the project and simply being a close friend who leads with encouragement. Also, a deep thank you to two special patients turned friends, Elise Daniel and Amber Joyce, for your brilliant ghostwriting, editing, and project-managing skills. You were both inside my heart and head, crystalizing my deepest truths and helping resolve many of the paradoxes and problems of doing so.

Big thanks go to Garrett Brown for helping us navigate the publishing landscape, and to my agent, Keeley Boeving at WordServe Literary, for championing the project. I am indebted to Keeley for much of the manuscript's polish as well as to friends who volunteered their time to provide invaluable feedback: Dr. Marie Anderson, Kathy Doherty, Sharon Chang, and Chaney.

To all the Tepeyac patients, many of whom drive long distances and send their daughters here for health care as they grow up and have their own children, thank you for choosing to see a medical team that humbly attempts to take their faith in the Risen Lord seriously in medicine. While on the subject of patients, I would like to mention that all patient names have been changed, along with most of the other names in my story.

I am grateful to all of the donors and prayer warriors from Tepeyac's early years to the present. You have all taught me much about the feminine genius, courage, commitment, and friendship. We were told we would not last a year in business, yet many of you sacrificed so much and got us through the ups and downs, enabling Tepeyac and Divine Mercy Care to be present for this time in our history.

Dr. Marie Anderson, Dr. Dan Fisk, Dr. Lorna Cvetkovitch, Dr. Miriam Pereira, Dr. Jenn Muldoon, Kim Terhune, and Victoria Snyder are on the front line and truly my brother and sisters in Christ. You have all sacrificed to join our practice. I am forever grateful for our conversations on "care and cure" and your friendship, support, and expertise.

Several others deserving mention are Shirley Warrick for her one-woman PR campaign in the early days and her intercessory prayers since; Bob, Gerry, and Cindy Laird, who have helped me understand what was at stake, what needed to happen practically, and how suffering strengthens one to embrace the grace of God to do what needs to get done to build a culture of life in this present environment; Ellen Curro, PA, who completed the integration in my training to care for the whole woman; the women wounded by abortion coming through our pregnancy resource centers, which were begun by Karen Shearer during my residency at the Witchduck Road Pregnancy Center; Dr. Paul McCauley, who gave me my first job and then taught me the art of communicating directly to patients their value and our friendship; my cousin Rob Roy McAnaw, who inspired me to pursue a dream and become a physician; Joe and Ronnie Januskievicz, who have interceded for me and truly held me close when I was facing many difficulties; Dr. Deborah Plumb, the NICU doctor who challenged me to care for two patients; and

Dr. David Kitay, who encouraged me to collaborate and serve female patients as an OB/GYN.

Finally, thank you to my sons, who have forgiven me for being away so much during their younger lives, and the love of my life and best friend, Carolyn. Without her, I'd still be a lukewarm man.

I

The One-Pound Person

It's another busy night in labor and delivery at Norfolk General Hospital. I hustle through the unit, which is abuzz with nurses, laboring mothers, and the rhythmic sounds of fetal heart monitors echoing into the hallway. I stop to check the patient chart hanging on the wall outside the delivery room to which I've been paged. I remove my watch, attach it to the drawstring of my scrubs, and get ready for a busy night delivering babies.

Inside, a woman lies trembling on a birthing bed with tears streaming down her cheeks as the nurse presses the button to tilt her backward. Her feet are raised higher than her head in an attempt to prevent what usually happens in these delivery rooms. She is in active preterm labor during her sixth month of pregnancy. At just 22 weeks' gestational age, my patient's son lacks the lung development to survive outside her womb, even with all the life-saving technology available to us in 1989. After examining the pages of her medical history chart, I explain her options. We could try to stop her contractions to give the baby a greater chance of survival, but she would risk contracting an intrauterine infection over the coming weeks, until her baby is ready to survive outside her

17

womb. Or, we can allow her labor to proceed naturally, potentially delivering a baby 18 weeks before his
due date. While many doctors and mothers might prefer
to allow nature to take its course in this situation, this
patient makes it clear that's not what she wants. And as
her doctor, I want whatever my patient wants. Together,
we will do everything possible to stop her labor and give
her the best pregnancy outcome.

I tell her I'm sending medication to slow her contractions through the IV attached to the back of her hand.
She's already five centimeters dilated, but if all goes as
planned, her contractions should stop within the hour.
Our eyes meet again. I see the fear and concern for the life
of her baby on her face. She nods and then turns to watch
the red-lined graph paper inching its way from the monitor beside her bed. A needle inside the machine records a
black line across the top of the page—the tiny, rapid heartbeat of her baby. *Buh bump, buh bump, buh bump.* She has
longed for the day when she will finally hold her child, but
tonight we are both determined to keep him safe inside
her womb.

Below her baby's heart rate, another line begins to
climb upward as the sudden wave of a new contraction
materializes and intensifies. She lets out a deep breath and
grips the bed rails on either side of her. I sense her reaction is not just from the physical pain of her labor, but
from her anticipation of the potential heartbreak the next
few moments may bring. When the contraction passes, I
turn to her with a smile and gently pat her arm. "Hang in
there," I tell her. "The meds will kick in soon." A cau-
tious peace softens her face as the tension begins to ease. I
take a step back, satisfied with our course of action to stop
her labor. A nurse peeks into the room. "Dr. Bruchalski,
you're needed next door."

"Try to relax," I remind the mother. "I'll be back shortly to check on you."

In an adjacent room, I greet a woman who also appears to be about five or six months pregnant. I glance at her intake paperwork: walk-in patient, no prenatal care. Her water began leaking earlier that morning, she tells me, but she is not in labor. I ask her the standard patient history questions: the date of her last menstrual cycle, whether or not this is her first pregnancy, if she has any allergies. She stares at the floor, mumbling her responses. She's either 21 or 22 weeks along, she can't remember, and I don't press her. "I just want it out," she demands, speaking directly for the first time.

I take note of her desire to terminate her pregnancy, so I breeze through the rest of her medical history. Of course, if she wanted to hear her options, I would be happy to explain them. I figure, given her history, she would have the choice to wait it out in the hospital for a few days to see if her body goes into labor naturally, almost certainly resulting in a miscarriage. If her body does not spontaneously go into labor, her second option would be to rest and wait patiently at home until the baby reaches a viable gestational age, about 26 weeks. In the meanwhile, it's possible that enough amniotic fluid would accumulate, and weeks later, after an extended hospital stay, she could deliver a healthy baby. If the fluid did not reaccumulate, it would affect the child's development and could result in disabilities. Both of these options could eventually lead to the delivery of a healthy child; however, they also carry the risk of infection and would require an extended hospital stay. But I assume she isn't interested in any of that, so I skip the explanations and the in-depth obstetric evaluation.

There's also a third route she could take—a route I've taken with patients many times before that doesn't risk intrauterine infection, delivering a disabled child, or a hefty hospital bill—an option I gather my patient might prefer: induce labor now. Inducing preterm labor on a previable fetus with some evidence that the mother is at risk for an infection is a legal, minimally invasive method to end a pregnancy, since the fetus is not yet old enough to survive outside the womb. I don't like to think of induction in this situation as an abortion, just the option in the best interest of the woman.

"I said, I just want it out," she repeats, visibly annoyed this time.

I decide to pull up a stool beside her bed to get a better understanding of her situation. A hollow stare fixes her attention on the wall in front of her when she tells me the pregnancy was unexpected. She wanted the baby at first, but now that her partner's commitment is fading, she can't imagine raising a child alone. Plus, a lengthy session of bedrest to keep her and her baby healthy until a safe delivery date is out of the question. She can't afford unexpected medical bills or the time away from work, which also rules out any interest in adoption. She's already had two abortions and figures, given her situation, she will have to do it again. My patient tells me she never wanted things to end up like this and just wants to leave this mess behind and move on with her life. She's had enough. Now staring down at her hands, my patient demands that I deliver and end the pregnancy, an option I am willing to provide.

I've worked with many women in similar situations, without the emotional or financial support they need to raise a child, and my heart breaks for her. My patient is in a position no woman ever wants to find herself in. In my assessment, I conclude that if we deliver the fetus today, its lungs will not be developed enough to breathe, even with oxygen assistance. Though I am always prepared to do everything in my power to save the lives of my patients' unborn babies, it's not what my patient wants today. I respect her decision and, considering all the circumstances outside of her control, understand why she thinks ending the pregnancy is her only choice.

I nod to the attending nurse, and she walks to the monitor beside my patient's bed and pushes the button to turn it off. We are taught as residents to spare the patient the sound of the heartbeat in these types of situations. An eerie silence takes the place of the once-steady beat of the fetal heart monitor. I break the silence to tell my patient we are adding Pitocin to her IV to jumpstart her contractions.

"Good," she says, "I have somewhere to be tonight."

She asks for an epidural. I her tell that I will get anesthesia for her and that I'm sorry things turned out this way. "You did all you could," I assure her, in hopes of easing the trauma of her decision.

My patient's contractions escalate quickly. Within a few hours, her cervix is dilated to 6 centimeters—just enough to deliver a fetus this small. The nursing staff transfers her onto a gurney and wheels her down the hall to a sterile operating room, in case any complications come up during delivery. They transfer her onto a bed and cradle her calves in stirrups. I roll my stool closer to her hips, position myself for delivery, and order her to push. She grabs her thighs and throws her shoulders forward, repeating the same movement with each contraction for two or three minutes. Then, the fetus and the placenta slide into my palms. I report to the nurse, "Done."

What I see in my hands induces more of a scientific curiosity than the joy of delivering a baby. The scrawny body begins at the tip of my fingers and ends at the middle of my wrist. Its wine-colored skin feels tacky and fragile,

not soft and supple like a baby's. Arms and legs jerk invol-
untarily. Eyes, sunken and closed. Mouth, gasping. And
then, a faint squeak.

We are required to resuscitate born-alive fetuses weighing over 500 grams, or about 1.1 pounds, at the hospital.
Medical experts believe a fetus at this weight has more than
a 20 percent chance of survival outside the womb. On the
basis of my experience and the quick history I took of my
patient, I was confident this one would be well under the
weight limit, since fetuses born at 21 or 22 weeks' gestation typically average only 400 grams [about 14 ounces]. I
had agreed to deliver—to terminate the pregnancy—under
the assumption that the patient's membranes had ruptured
many hours ago and she was most likely getting infected; I
was relatively certain that resuscitation would not be necessary, since I believed the fetus would pass away during
the stresses of labor. I had expected to give my patient
basic post-stay instructions and send her home, both of us
accepting the unfortunate reality that abortion had been
her only realistic option. But that is not what happened.

I stand up, wiping blood and birth fluids on my delivery gown. Cradling the fetus in the palm of my hand, I
walk over to the scale. With my right hand, I zero the
machine, pick him up by the skull, and lay him down
without the blue "chuck" pad used to protect babies from
the scale's cold platform. The red numerals flash 505 grams
[17.8 ounces].

My stomach drops. I lunge toward the emergency button to alert the neonatal intensive care unit and immediately turn on the warmer. My patient must have been
further along in her pregnancy than she thought, maybe
24 weeks. Maybe *more*. The limit of viability is considered to be 24 weeks, meaning abortion is illegal in Virginia after this point because the fetus would have at least

a 50 percent chance of survival outside the womb. I think back to our intake conversation and realize that after learning my patient wanted an abortion, I breezed over important questions that might have pointed to a more mature pregnancy. I failed to perform the usual in-depth obstetric evaluation, which includes bloodwork and an ultrasound that would have depicted her baby's anatomy, assessed the amount of amniotic fluid present, and, most importantly, established her baby's estimated fetal weight as being more than expected for the 21–22 week dates my patient had given me and on which I had based my treatment. The knowledge that her baby was older than she had led me to believe would have dramatically changed my obstetric management.

I consider myself a good resident and a rule-following guy, but the details of my patient's pregnancy seemed unimportant to me after learning she didn't want to carry to term—and knowing I could offer her the solution. I hope following the emergency protocol will compensate for the poor history I procured. I leave the fetus on the scale and return to my patient to check her vitals and make sure she's not hemorrhaging.

Suddenly, the delivery room door swings open. Dr. Deborah Plumb hurries toward me. Between her natural height and her moral uprightness, she is an imposing figure, and she seems to tower over me as she approaches. Known among the physicians at the hospital for her medical excellence and thorough evaluations, Dr. Plumb is one of the best and brightest neonatologists on staff. Her vast knowledge has always intimidated me, and the few words she has typically spoken have commanded my complete attention.

Following close on her heels, Dr. Plumb's entourage rushes into the room: a nurse, a nurse practitioner, and a pediatric resident. A chill from the door's breeze hits my face. It has been an unfortunate turn of events that they even need to respond to my call in the first place. I chalk my mistake up to a minor technicality and wait for Dr. Plumb to sign off on it.

"This one's just over 500," I tell her.

She glares at me and begins asking questions about the mother's history. I have few answers. She rushes to the warmer to assess the baby's vital signs. Every second is precious for an extremely premature baby to be success-fully resuscitated, and this one is about 6 pounds below the average weight of a full-term newborn. I return to clean up my patient, who is confused about all the hubbub surrounding the delivery. My handling of the situation was poor form and I knew it. I should have considered the likelihood of delivering a viable fetus more carefully, though at this moment, I just wish he had weighed a few grams less to save myself this humiliation.

Dr. Plumb remains calm as she oversees the pediatric resident intubating the fetus to begin the flow of oxygen into his severely underdeveloped lungs. With command-ing professionalism, she calls for a transport team to rush the fetus to the NICU. She kneels next to the patient to explain what's happening, then pulls me aside. "Stop giv-ing me tumors, John."

"What?"

"Stop treating these babies like they're tumors. You're better than that. You're a *good* physician."

Her words suck the oxygen from my lungs. My head begins to spin. The commotion around me falls to mur-murs, and colors dim to gray. Her brows furrow and lips move, but I cannot make out what she is saying. *Tumors? As in, cancerous tumors? Do I really treat unwanted fetuses like tumors needing to be removed from my patients?*

"Did you hear me, John? The mother shouldn't be your only concern in these delivery rooms. You have two patients, not just one."

The door shuts behind her. I take a step backward and grip the metal railing on the delivery bed to steady myself. Her words reverberate in my head. "Stop giving me tumors. You're better than that, John."

I wonder if I have been practicing a double standard. Why was I doing everything I could in one room to save the life of an unborn baby, but so quick and willing to get rid of another one in the room next door? Was my standard for life really based on whether the mother wanted the child inside her womb?

I had wanted to be a doctor, to be a *good* doctor, since I was a teenager. I'd always desired to care for the sick and problem-solve complex medical issues. I also trusted women, and I wanted to make life better for them. And that's what I had thought I was doing. I had given each mother exactly what she wanted, so why was I so torn up about this? Sure, I should have taken a more thorough medical history, but there was something deeper bothering me, something I couldn't quite pinpoint. All I knew was that I felt like I had caught a whack in the gut from a baseball bat. Dr. Plumb's piercing words echoed in my head again, and I knew, somehow, that I would never be the same.

2

The Visible Man

A light dusting of snow covered the driveway of our single-level home, but I never let a little snow stop me from my after-school basketball routine. I dropped my backpack by the front door and threw on my sweatpants, a gray hooded sweatshirt, and my knock-off Chuck Taylor high tops. I pulled a glove over my left hand, leaving my shooting hand free. I shoveled away a patch of snow large enough to practice my foul shots.

Sports didn't come as easily to me as it did to my two more athletic and better-looking brothers. I was shorter than the other 12-year-old boys in my class and couldn't jump very high, and I'll just say I wore "husky" boys' clothing from Sears. Between my build and my asthma, my speed suffered the most. During practice drills, I ran like I had a piano on my back. I even earned the nickname Turtle from my teammates.

I cupped my hands over my mouth. A frosty puff of breath escaped through my fingers. Taking the basketball on my fingertips, I bent my knees, zeroed in on the center of the backboard, jumped, and released. The shot was good, and I wouldn't quit until I shot 19 more in a row just like it.

The rumble of my dad's 1969 Volkswagen Beetle sounded in the distance. You could always hear that car before you could see it, its gears grinding as it lurched down Martis Place and rounded the corner onto Reid Court. We affectionately named my dad's car The *Maslanka*, which means "buttermilk" in Polish, for its creamy off-white color. The Maslanka pulled into the hedge-lined driveway, leaving a trail of arctic exhaust in its path. Its tires crunched the snow as it pulled to a stop at the bottom of the driveway to give me plenty of shooting space for my imaginary foul line.

The driver-side door creaked open, and Dad stepped out in his gray, crumpled trench coach and brimmed hat, looking right at me through his glasses. I knew from his expression that something was wrong. Disappointment was spread across his face. "Johnny, today is Black Monday!"

I watched another shot sink into the basket. "What do you mean?"

"Our nation just legalized abortion."

"What's that?"

"It's killing an unborn child, Johnny. It's now legal to take the life of an unborn baby in this country, in the United States of America!"

"Oh ..." I jumped for another shot. The ball circled the hoop, which quickly ejected it, and landed in a bush. Dad stuffed a stack of papers under one arm, grabbed his briefcase with his other, and hurried inside to continue his rant with Mom.

Dad called the day the Supreme Court ruled abortion to be a woman's constitutional right "Black Monday" because he considered it an irredeemable turning point in America's history. (Dad was not, of course, referring to the global stock market crash of 1987, which also happened on a Monday. That Black Monday was still over 14 years in the future when he coined the phrase.) To him, January 22, 1973, represented a total abandonment of morality. Legalizing abortion was a denial of natural human rights, a betrayal of our nation's most vulnerable citizens. This nation, founded on the Judeo-Christian belief that human life is sacred because man is created in the image of God, had just legalized killing babies in the sanctum of their mothers' wombs. Once a nation sanctioned such a grave evil, it was doomed to implode, he thought. What struck me most on that cold day in January was not the gravity of the court ruling, but the sorrow on my father's face and how long it remained.

When I was 12, *Roe v. Wade* didn't have much significance in my life. I was more concerned with basketball tryouts than politics, which was all the subject of abortion seemed to be at the time—a legal issue. What I didn't realize was that the Supreme Court decision would forever change the nation I'd live in and the social pressures of the medical field I'd one day enter. It would callous and erode my conscience and grant me the world's stamp of approval when I would one day be asked to stop a beating heart. Along with the seven justices who voted in favor of *Roe*, I, too, would eventually betray my faith and my father, as well as the millions of unborn American babies he deemed worthy of protection.

Above Dad's blackboard at Don Bosco Prep, where he taught civics, hung a ten-foot-long poster with a Daniel Webster quote in large black letters: "Whatever makes men good Christians, makes them good citizens." There was no distinction between good Christians and good citizens in Dad's eyes, and he took both his faith and his politics very seriously. In 1969 he received the Valley Forge Teacher's Medal, an award for educators who did an exceptional job "teaching patriotic citizenship and an understanding of the spiritual, constitutional, and moral value of our constitutional republic."[1] To him, legalizing abortion was an absolute repudiation of America's founding principles, a true loss of Christian morals. Governance and faith could not be separated in one's private or public life. Neither good Christians nor good citizens could possibly allow something as horrific as abortion to creep into society's canon of socially acceptable behavior.

My father's parents left Poland for America before World War I to escape the battle zone in search of a better life. My father, Thaddeus Bruchalski (Tadj or Ted for short), was the oldest of five boys, born at home in 1923. His Polish roots left him feeling personally connected to the atrocities the Poles suffered under Nazi occupation and, later, Soviet rule. Dad had been particularly moved by the Poles' loss of their freedom of religion, which was my father's most cherished freedom of the American Constitution. Saddened to learn that many of his Christian friends and relatives were forced to practice their faith in private or face persecution by Stalin, Dad prayed every day for the conversion of Russia from communism. He made friends with Hungarian refugees who had escaped Budapest during the anticommunist revolt in 1956 and regularly invited them to his home for meals as he helped them find jobs and a community.

At a time when he saw faith and American public policy growing ever more distant from each other, Dad truly lived the quote on his classroom wall. He always made it a point to vote, engage in political discussion, help people in need, and pray for those suffering under corrupt

---

[1] "The Valley Forge Teacher's Medal", *Deseret News Salt Lake Telegram*, October 28, 1959, 18A, 7.

governments. Now, he added the holocaust of the unborn in America to his daily prayers. He'd pray with us every night before bed, pleading God for mercy on our nation and for the conversion of people involved in abortion.

After serving in World War II, Dad joined his Uncle Joseph, known to the community as Father Haluch, at Don Bosco Prep. Father Haluch ran the school and also served as pastor of the Immaculate Heart of Mary Catholic Church. He invited Dad to play the organ for Sunday Masses, and Dad organized a choir to accompany him. One of the altos, a petite, spunky brunette, would later accompany him for life.

To make up for his humble teacher's salary, Dad moonlighted as a security guard, from six to eleven o'clock. He was the last one to bed in our family and the first one awake. For our 6:30 A.M. wake-up call, he would knock on our bedroom doors ten minutes early. "Rise and shine!" His early morning cheerfulness was usually met with grumbles as we buried ourselves further beneath our blankets. When we emerged from our rooms, Dad would lead the family in morning prayer, always asking God to deliver Russia from communism. We would eat our oatmeal while watching *The Little Rascals* and then pile into The Maslanka to go to school.

The choirgirl who had stolen Dad's heart and ended his bachelorhood was Veronica Janisheski. Like him, she was from a family of Polish Catholic immigrants who left Central Europe shortly before World War I. Mom was the fifth of nine brothers and sisters, all born and raised in Mahwah, with the exception of my Uncle Bill, who was born in the middle of the Atlantic Ocean on a ship bound for New York. Mom's father was a butcher, just like Dad's father, and the owner of Janek's Meat Market. My parents began dating in 1958 and married in 1959, and

I arrived the following year in September. Mom told me the story of my birth many times: I was born *en caul*, with a fully intact amniotic sac over my head—an extremely rare occurrence—arriving safely with the help of forceps. She gave birth to my brother Paul three years later and my youngest brother, Tommy, the year after that.

I admired my parents for their faith, especially Mom. While she was not always physically strong, her spiritual strength was unmatched by any woman I knew. She was a prayer warrior who prayed every day for her brothers and cousins who were recovering from alcoholism and her sisters who battled cancer. And she prayed faithfully for my brothers and me. I remember her pacing at my baseball games, when I threw relief pitches and the bases were loaded, her head bowed, eyes closed, lips silently mouthing a prayer for me. Though not as vocal as Dad about her faith, she prayed diligently for the intentions on her heart.

Mom loved her boys but knew we were God's boys first. After my baptism, she told me she had offered me to God, saying, "We give him to you. Take him as your son and teach him." She thought of God as a father and knew he cared deeply for her and watched over her family. Her faith was not particularly intellectual; rather, it sprang from a deeply personal and intimate relationship with her Creator. I believe it was her faith in God's saving grace and her persevering prayers for me that helped lead me to the most transformational and providential moment of my life many years later.

Emotionally, Mom was incredibly resilient. It was Dad, not Mom, who was inconsolable the morning my brother Paul was shot at the drugstore by a thug looking for cash. Mom remained focused and levelheaded, choosing me to go to the hospital because I was the eldest and had a good understanding of medicine. Paul's wound was a clean-through flesh wound, and the bullet did not touch his femur or any major blood vessels. (I imagine Mom's incessant praying for God to protect her boys helped make sure of it.) But what I remember most about that day was how calm Mom remained in a crisis situation that easily could have sent any parent into a panic.

Reid Court, where we grew up, was overrun by Jani-sheski cousins playing hide-and-go-seek and pranks on the neighbors. When we weren't ding-dong ditching their homes or leaving flaming bags of dog poop at their feet, we were mowing their lawns to make up for it. Our bike brigade could be seen pedaling on the side of the road, on a mission to buy penny candy at the Country Store on Saturdays. When Mom picked us up from grammar school, she let ten of us cram in The Maslanka with four of us in the back seat, three in the back trunk, and three packed in the front seat. But she drew the line at stuffing my little cousin Chris in the front trunk.

Mom's health was poor. She was asthmatic like me, and when she lay in bed with her back pain, I sympathized. I admired Dad for dutifully stepping into the role of caregiver whenever Mom wasn't feeling well. He would tell her to stay in bed in the mornings while he got Paul, Tommy, and me ready and off to school. I believe it was through a combination of watching Dad care for Mom so graciously and my parents' complementary loving gestures toward me when I was sick that I learned how to care for patients with genuine love and tenderness.

One early experience that uncovered my calling to medicine happened at my cousin Rob's house in Virginia when I was eight years old. Rob had quite a collection of model cars, tanks, submarines, and airplanes, which I sometimes helped him to build. But one day, I saw a different kind of model displayed on the shelf above his desk: a plastic human body, standing about 10 inches tall, staring back at me. The Visible Man Anatomy Kit had removable organ pieces, which could be seen through its transparent outer shell.

Rob was eight years older than I, and I always regarded him as a surrogate older brother and adopted many of his interests. On our next visit to the hobby shop, I bought a Visible Man model just like his. Later, I purchased the Visible Woman and also the pregnant Visible Woman. My heart filled with wonder as I turned the tiny plastic womb around in my fingers, examining the unborn baby inside.

In the years that followed, I developed an intense desire to learn everything I could about the human body. I bought every medical model I could afford, including human heart and lung replicas, with tooth fairy change, birthday money from my grandparents, and the dollar bills Mom slipped me for doing chores. My parents (and Santa) encouraged my fascination with human biology by leaving new models under the Christmas tree. The only thing my parents did not encourage was Rob's and my tendency to label body parts with permanent marker on my little brother Tommy's skin while he was sleeping. It became somewhat of an art form—how quietly we could sneak up on him, how carefully we could write without caus-ing him to stir, and how many body parts we could label before he'd wake up screaming when he saw the words "thigh", "knee", and "calf" written down his legs.

In the fifth grade, I proudly turned in a five-page essay entitled "Why I Want to Be a Doctor". In the paper, I described my fascination with human organs and how they miraculously work together to keep a person alive. Two years earlier, in third grade, I had brought a How and Why Wonder Book on the human body to school.

When I opened the book during breaks, a circle of my peers formed around me as I pointed to pictures of week-by-week fetal development. One of the Felician Sisters who ran Immaculate Heart of Mary Grammar School slapped me on the wrist for bringing inappropriate material to class. She did not approve of the pictures depicting early embryonic cells dividing to form human life, because they elicited thoughts of reproduction. Years later, I confessed to a priest that I had despised nuns for the remainder of my childhood because of that incident.

Despite my attitude toward religious sisters, we were a very devout Catholic family. When one of the Bruchalski brothers was signed up for altar service, we would wake up before the sun and load into The Maslanka. Arriving on time for the 6:30 daily Mass was especially trying during dark winter mornings, because the car did not have a heater. Tommy, Paul, and I would wipe our hands on the windows to defrost them before leaving for church. We looked forward to the warm, fresh roll at Janek's that Dad would get us on the way to school after Mass.

I enjoyed serving as an altar boy, especially at the Sunday Masses when my brothers and I all served together with Dad's uncle, Father Haluch. The 15-foot crucifix that hung from the church ceiling above the altar easily subdued me into an attitude of reverence. Whenever I gazed up at Christ's face, I imagined myself present at the Crucifixion, wanting so desperately to relieve his pain, the pain that I had contributed to when he bore the weight of my sin. My parents taught me to read Scripture with fresh eyes, as if every time was my first time reading that passage, and to picture myself there, with Jesus.

Pictures in our home helped center my heart on Christ as well. One image depicted the resurrected Christ with his heart visible, which reminded me of my Visible Man models. The painting showed that his heart had been lacerated, as described by the Gospel of John: "But one of the soldiers pierced his side with a spear, and at once there came out blood and water" (19:34). (I later learned the medical explanation for the water: the rupture of the pericardium membrane wrapped around his heart.) In the painting, Jesus holds one hand to his heart and one stretched out in loving invitation. I spent a lot of time studying this image, the twisted thorns around his heart, the drops of blood below the wound, and the loving gaze of my Savior.

In those early years, it was easy to focus my heart on Christ. I prayed to him almost every day and often contemplated his ultimate sacrifice—and how undeserving I was of salvation. Most importantly for me as a young boy, Jesus was a friend I knew I could always count on. But, as I would soon find out, abiding in Christ and cherishing the nearness of his friendship would not always come easily to me. At 12 I was a bright-eyed kid, excited about the potential in the world around me, about fitting in with my friends and making the basketball team. The reverence for Christ I had felt at an early age slowly began to wane as I entered adolescence and began to question what I had been taught by my parents and my faith about right and wrong.

3

Weighing the Pros and the Cons

1974

Dad made sure that my brothers' and my hair was always short and neat. To Dad, "neat" meant our hair was above the ear and off the collar and parted on the side. All I knew was that "neat" wasn't cool. All my friends were growing their hair out, and I wanted to, too. But Dad didn't want us to resemble any of the Woodstock hippies we saw walking on the side of the road when we drove through upstate New York on our way to Canada for a vacation during that "Summer of Love".

To appease Dad, I ended up keeping my hair neater than the hippies', though I loved listening to what he thought of as hippie music. Fleetwood Mac's album *Rumors* was always playing on my cassette player. Dad, of course, said the music I listened to was just "banging noise". His musical taste was rigid and respectable, just like his hair standards. When Mom and I were watching the Beatles perform live on TV, Dad grumbled his way into the living room to complain. He shouted at the TV as he threw his hands in the air in bewilderment.

But the cultural rebellion of the era ran deeper than hair and music. Young people challenged major institutions, protested the Vietnam War, fought for civil rights, and overhauled the social and political landscape. The hard-working, conservative post–World War II era in which Dad had grown up, when immigrants pledged their allegiance through service and sacrifice, was being replaced. Young people, fed up with the wartime trends of the age, searched for peace through musical and artistic expression. I wasn't aware of it at the time, but in the 1960s and 1970s, tradition gave way to progressivism, and truth gave way to relativism.

Change swept over the culture like a tidal wave—and reached the Catholic pews as well.

The year before I was born, in 1959, Pope John XXIII announced that the bishops of the Roman Catholic Church would gather in Rome for the Second Vatican Council. The announcement, which was accompanied by the idea that the Church needed some updating, shocked the world, and I imagine it shocked my Dad more than most. The pope said that the goal of the Council was to find ways to present Catholic teaching and practice more efficaciously—and more mercifully. While Dad agreed this was a noble pursuit, some of the ways the Council was implemented felt radical to him.

Dad was most disturbed by the changes made to Catholic worship. For example, we were allowed to receive Communion standing rather than kneeling and in the hand rather than on the tongue. During Mass, instead of facing the altar (and God) along with the congregation, the priest was now allowed to stand behind the altar, facing the people. To Dad, this turned the focus from Christ and us before the Father to us alone. He saw these changes, along with the folk music and the increasingly casual clothes young people would wear to church, as signs of disrespect to our Lord. He thought that Mass was becoming more about how relevant the Church could be to the modern world rather than worshipping and showing reverence to God.

While Dad mourned the loss of many traditions, others welcomed the changes. Journalists attended the Council proceedings and shared their opinions with the world through newspapers, magazines, radio, and television. Pope John XXIII was even chosen as *Time*'s 1962 Man of the Year. For perhaps the first time in history, the world could observe the Catholic Church through the lens of the mass media, and that visibility gave some people the impression that the Church was on the brink of changing her moral teachings.

After all, some Church positions, such as forbidding contraception, seemed outdated to many modern people both inside and outside the Church. If the Church could change the Mass, why couldn't it change other things as well? In fact, many Catholics looked forward to changes in the Church's moral teachings that they considered inevitable.

One of my high school religion teachers at Don Bosco Prep challenged our all-boys class with an ethical question. Father Coccelli asked us to picture ourselves all grown up with a wife and kids and a house, living in the middle of a war zone. He told us to imagine the enemy looting stores and robbing houses in town while we were on lockdown at home to protect our family. And then one night, something terrible happens.

"Armed enemy soldiers break into your house. One of them grabs your wife and holds her at gunpoint," he told us. "Then, he looks you in the eye and asks you if you are a Christian. He promises to kill your wife if you say yes." Father Coccelli paused to let the scenario sink in. Then he asked, "Should you deny Christ to save your wife?"

I was always quick to raise my hand with an answer, but this exercise had me stumped. A few of my classmates looked in my direction, waiting. A long moment of silence passed before our teacher volunteered the answer: "Well, when you consider the grave ramifications of answering yes, the most virtuous option would be to save your wife." Father Coccelli claimed that in this case, a lie is the "lesser of the two evils". "Christ forgives those who deny him," he said. "He knows that you really love him and that you are in a difficult situation. He knows that you did your best in balancing your options. Have faith in his mercy." He went on to say that when we're faced with morally difficult situations like the scenario he described, we should weigh the pros and the cons and choose the lesser of two evils. What really matters, he said, is your heart.

His explanation seemed logical to me at the time, but it was wrong. One must never choose an evil, even if it is "lesser". I knew this in my heart, but I didn't have the words or the courage to articulate it at the time. I knew that I should never deny my Lord and Savior, no matter what the cost. Christ said we are to love him even more than our own family, even more than our own lives (Mt 10:37; 16:25). Yes, God is forgiving. But his forgiveness doesn't turn an evil action into a good one. In fact, the need for forgiveness shows the action was evil, whether it was done out of weakness or malice.

The idea that we should do our best and "God would understand" was something I and many of my Catholic peers had heard before. I think some priests became afraid of turning people away from the Catholic Church by preaching too much about sin and hell. Whenever the topic of sin came up in Confirmation class at church or my religion classes in school, the nuns would assure us that God is understanding of our sins. God's love was emphasized while our sinfulness was downplayed. Unfortunately, these teachers failed to demonstrate that the Gospel is about both—the desperate state of my sinful nature, despite my best intentions, and the overwhelming love of Christ that nailed my sin to a cross and exchanged it for a spotless record before God.

In contrast to my teachers, my parents, raised in the orthodoxy of Polish Catholicism, put a heavy emphasis on following the rules, to keep us *out* of sin: Go to Confession. Serve as altar boys. Always genuflect toward the tabernacle when you are entering or exiting your pew. The message of the importance of having a personal relationship with Christ, the message I needed most, was not coming through. There was much more talk about how to be a "good Catholic", and so that's where my focus remained. As a result, Mass became merely a weekly ritual, a going through the motions, despite the Second Vatican Council's attempts to help Catholics avoid this pitfall.

Meanwhile, I still enjoyed praying occasionally and singing hymns at Mass on Sunday mornings, but spending time with God became secondary to other things in my life, such as playing baseball and hanging out with friends. Though I appeared to be a faithful Catholic on the outside, my heart was far from God.

Every year in January after that snowy day when Dad announced it was Black Monday, he took a busload of boys from Don Bosco Prep to the March for Life in Washington, D.C. The annual rally on the national mall draws hundreds of thousands of pro-life advocates who gather to protest the legality of abortion. Dad feared the Church was growing fragile in the face of political upheaval since Catholics, and their fellow Christians, couldn't stop the *Roe v. Wade* decision. "Gone are the days of Christians living their faith in the public square," he would lament. Participating in the March for Life was the way he chose to live out *his* faith in the public square. Though I saw how important civic engagement was to him and how broken his heart was over the abortion issue, I never joined him at a March for Life, and he never asked me to.

Maybe Dad never asked me to come to the March for Life because he could tell I didn't care about it. It wasn't that I disagreed that unborn children should be protected; I just didn't think about it much. In my mind, abortion was a women's issue, and no one my age was talking about it. My thoughts were consumed with whether I'd throw a wild pitch at our next baseball game or if I'd get a chance to talk to the girl I had a crush on after practice.

Still, I remember clearly the first time the topic of abortion came up in the locker room. One of my buddies on the baseball team, whom we called Miller, confided in me and a few of our teammates that he'd gotten his girlfriend pregnant. Though I didn't know Miller's girlfriend well, hearing that news was uncomfortable. No one ever talked about getting pregnant, and I certainly had never known anyone my age who was.

Another teammate made a suggestion to Miller. "You know, it's really not a big deal. You can pay to have that taken care of." We all knew what he was talking about. Miller shook his head. He wasn't interested in that option. A rare silence descended on our corner of the locker room.

Then, in an attempt to lighten the mood, our teammate blurted out, "What would you do if you got someone knocked up, Bruch?" I laughed reluctantly at his teasing and changed the subject.

The topic of girls had come up many times before in that boys' locker room. I did my best to tune out the debates about which girls were more attractive and the one-upmanship surrounding taking girls on dates and sleeping with them. Conversations that objectified women came easily to teenage boys. But when it came to the realities of our newfound sexuality, such as getting your girlfriend pregnant and what to do about it, those conversations were awkward—shameful, even, like a dirty secret. They would pop up momentarily and then disappear into the background even faster than they had come. When our teammate told Miller he could get the pregnancy taken care of, he didn't even use the word "abortion". These topics hid in the shadows and were not discussed openly among my peers. I don't remember the matter coming up again.

I never heard if Miller's girlfriend had the baby or not, and I never asked—probably because I didn't want to know. I imagined that whether she had the baby or had an abortion, the silence of the time regarding the issues would have garnered an equal measure of shame and isolation. The tragedy of it all, to me, was that no matter how she handled the reality of her pregnancy, she would have to grow up much faster than the rest of us.

I thought back to the Visible Woman models I used to explore with my cousin Rob and how I'd stare at the tiny baby inside the pregnant model's uterus in total wonderment. Perhaps it had more to do with my interest in human biology and amazement at the human reproductive system, but knowing one of the girls in my group of friends had been pregnant left a lasting impression on me. I began to consider the girls in my life in a more thoughtful and respectful way.

The girls I knew trusted me. For starters, I wasn't interested in sleeping around like some of the other guys on the team. By my own standards, I was a good kid who tried to follow the rules that I learned at home and in church, and not sleeping around was one of those rules. The girls knew I respected them, and so they shared openly with me. My friend Galina once confided in me about her fear of not being able to have children.

I suppose many adolescent boys would have squirmed at the topic, but she knew about my love for human biology and my desire to become a doctor one day. I listened and asked questions when she shared that she'd recently been diagnosed with ovarian cysts and suffered terribly from pain and bleeding caused by them. While friends vented their frustrations with their parents, Mom confided in me about the challenges of Dad working all the time. Female relatives told me about their marital and relationship issues. I was a naturally good listener and problem solver, and I loved knowing I was helping those close to me by offering a listening ear and a compassionate heart.

Even when I was young, God was at work in my heart, preparing me for a future vocation as an OB/GYN. Little by little, he was exposing me to women's health issues and teaching me to build respectful relationships with female friends. I was beginning to appreciate the intricacies and depth of the female spirit. Looking back now, I see that through these conversations, God was expanding my understanding of women and the biological and relationship challenges they face. Now and then, I thought about medical school, but that was still a long way away. For the time being, I had my sights set on soaking up all the freedoms of my last real summer vacation.

1978–1982

I let my hair grow long the moment I left home for my freshman year of college. I was finally free from Dad's rigid standards and compulsive crew cuts, and my hair was free to grow past the bridge of my nose. I also started parting it in the middle—something Dad hated about unkempt '70s hair—and finally grew the beard I had been wanting for years, sparse as it may have been.

Dad wouldn't like my new look, and I knew it. When I came home the first time for Thanksgiving, he took one look at me and blurted out, "What?!" Stunned, all he could do was stare at my beard, and then my hair, and back at my beard again. Mom was quick with an elbow jab to his side as she pushed past him to wrap me in a big welcome-home hug.

I had chosen Spring Hill College, a private Catholic liberal arts school in Mobile, Alabama. Dad was pleased I had chosen to continue a Catholic education and thought the genteel southern culture would provide a positive influence during my young-adult years. Plus, their renowned biology program promised to prepare me well for medical school, if I decided to walk down that road. Either way, I knew I loved studying the human body, and I was up for the challenge. The biology department at Spring Hill was known for leaving only the best and brightest students standing on graduation day. Only a dozen of the nearly hundred students who enrolled as freshmen were expected to make it through until the end. I knew that if I could survive, I would have a good shot at getting into medical school.

The culture around the campus was what you might expect from the Deep South: lots of Baptist churches, lots of old money, and lots of Republicans. Dad thought sending me to a Catholic college in the South meant I would be surrounded by clean-cut, proper, conservative Christians, but that was not exactly the case. The Jesuit priests and brothers who taught classes on campus were what my father would call "liberal Catholics". They were against the Vietnam War and seemed to talk more about "social justice" than about Jesus Christ. Many of them were distrustful of

Pope John Paul II and his orthodox explanations of Catholic teaching.

Pope John Paul II, who was elected in 1978, was known for being a "conservative pope". He condemned abortion as part of the "culture of death" and opposed contraception (though he supported fertility awareness–based methods of family planning). He denounced communism, which had spread rapidly throughout Eastern Europe after the Cold War and had taken hold of his home country of Poland. I imagine my Polish, orthodox, and communism-hating father and Pope John Paul II would have gotten along well.

Pope John Paul II also expressed reservations about "liberation theology", which was popular in Latin America at the time and in the lecture halls of Spring Hill College. Liberation theology was a controversial teaching because it joined Marxist economic theory with Christian theology. Liberation theology did so in reaction to social injustice in Latin America and out of the belief that society should confront the deplorable conditions of the poor first and foremost. The theology suggests the focus of Christ's ministry was to uplift, enrich, and liberate the *materially* poor, rather than to heal all of mankind's spiritual poverty—and my professors seemed to endorse this perspective. Dad would have considered these ideas radical and heretical, a complete twisting of the message of the Gospel to fit popular opinions of the time. I occasionally wondered what he would have thought if he knew I was learning all about the merits and virtues of Marxist-inspired theology in class while he was at home praying for the fall of communism in Eastern Europe.

My Catholic professors pushed a theory that I'd first been introduced to in my religion classes in high school: proportionalism, a popular teaching in Catholic education during the 1960s and 1970s. Proportionalism is an ethical theory which holds that no moral norms bind absolutely. It says that one should weigh all the good and evil that could result from different actions and choose the action that brings about the greater good.

In my biology ethics class, we ran through several ethical thought experiments like Father Coccelli's scenario, simplifying hard choices through the use of proportionalism. A stranded raft floats in the middle of the ocean with an old man, a young mother, a businessman, a Marine, and food enough for only three of them to survive until rescue. Who sacrifices himself for the benefit of the others? Or a pregnant mother falls comatose at 38 weeks' gestation. Only she or her full-term baby will survive delivery. Whose life do you prioritize?

In thinking through these hypothetical scenarios, I was often stumped. There didn't seem to be a right answer. But the message of proportionalism is that it can sometimes be right to do an action that presents itself as morally wrong. This is a controversial teaching for an orthodox Catholic, because it holds that no action is actually intrinsically evil, and because it bases moral decisions on personal conscience rather than on biblical principles or Church teaching on morality and virtue.[1] The Church teaches that a good intention does not make an intrinsically disordered behavior good or just,[2] and Pope John Paul II criticized proportionalism in later encyclical letters in the 1990s.

Although I was experiencing it firsthand, I did not fully comprehend that after Vatican II, there was a rift between

---

[1] The ethical theory of proportionalism contradicts the teaching of *The Catechism of the Catholic Church*, no. 1756 (hereafter cited as CCC); see also John Paul II, encyclical letter *Veritatis splendor* (The Splendor of Truth) (August 6, 1993), nos. 47, 78, and 80; and Vatican Council II, Pastoral Constitution on the Church in the Modern World *Gaudium et spes* (December 7, 1965), no. 27.

[2] CCC no. 1756.

Catholic academia and the Magisterium of the Catholic Church. Catholic professors believed they had the moral responsibility to debate and even reject Church teachings in the name of progress and academic freedom, and the professors at my school were no exception.

While I was exposed to so many new ways of thinking in college, I didn't want to adhere to any particular ideology. I was never a very radical thinker, or a very political one, so I decided to remain undecided. Neutral. Open-minded. Instead of trying to poke holes in my professors' arguments, I wanted to appreciate them, or at least find certain aspects with which I could agree. Occasionally when I did disagree, I "disagreed agreeably", as Dad would say. I wanted to please my professors, and I didn't want to cause any conflict in the classroom.

There was one time I tried to poke a hole in my professor's position, though. In one of my situational ethics classes, Father Carran often made a case for moral relativism by arguing that since everyone has a different perception of reality, we are unable to come to an agreement on what reality really is. Therefore, truth will always be relative to each person's perception and will differ from one person to the next.

When I told Dad over the phone what I was learning in class, he shipped a book to my campus mailing address and instructed me to read it immediately. *Right and Reason: Ethics in Theory and Practice* by Father Austin Fagothey arrived one week later. I brought it to my next situational ethics class, and the next time Father Carran began pontificating about moral relativism, I flipped to some of the pages Dad had dog-eared. I found the quote I was searching for and raised my hand.

"Yes, John."

"I've been reading a book on morality and ethics, and the author claims that if all truth is relative and there is

no absolute truth, then believing in anything, even relativism, can't be possible. So doesn't that disprove moral
relativism?"

He tilted his nose down and stared at me over the frames
of his glasses. "Boy, John, you're asking some interesting
questions today." He paused for a moment, and then the
bell rang.

I closed my book, feeling both embarrassed for questioning my professor and annoyed that he hadn't given me
an answer. I worried that he thought I was stupid. What
frustrated me the most, though, was how unsure I myself
was about the truth. What *is* truth? I had been taught
that truth exists and that if I follow Christ's teachings, I
will know the truth (Jn 8:31–32). There was truth to be
known, and in the depths of my soul I knew this. But that
day in class, it all seemed so complicated.

Only one of my professors did not subscribe to moral
relativism and proportionalism: Dr. Bonhoffitz. He was a
Lutheran of Jewish heritage who taught philosophy and
loved Pope John Paul II. I enrolled in his class on phenomenological realism, a philosophy that searches for
objectivity in topics that are usually regarded as subjective
and insists on the subject's ability to come into contact
with the truth directly through his experience.

"Let's talk about a dog," he announced to the class one
day. "John, what's your definition of a dog?"

"It's a four-legged mammal of the *Canis* genus," I said.

"Very good. Jimmy, what's a dog?" He asked every student in the class to define a dog and each one of us gave a
different answer. "Sue, what's a dog to you?"

Sue described the poodle she had owned growing up,
the fluffiness of his white fur and how much she had loved
him. Then she turned the question to our professor. "Dr.
Bonhoffitz, what does a dog mean to you?"

He walked up to her desk and bent down to meet her at eye level. He pulled up the cuff on his sleeve and showed her the six-digit number tattooed on his forearm. "It's the animal that killed my mother and father. A German soldier let a wild dog loose on them at Auschwitz and it mauled my mother right in front of me. I hate dogs."

Dr. Bonhoffitz's demonstration was to show that we all have different experiences with dogs, and those experiences flavor our ideas of what a dog really is. If you had watched a wild dog kill someone you loved, you'd hate dogs, too. Your experience matters—but it's not the only thing that matters. Regardless of our subjective interactions with dogs, there is also a truth about dogs that is independent of our experience of them, like that dogs have four legs and they're carnivores. What was so helpful about the phenomenological perspective was that it didn't insist that one must choose between the importance of experience and objective truth; it held that absolute truth could be found while still validating our personal perceptions. Phenomenological realism protected truth, while the philosophies many of my other professors pushed, such as proportionalism and relativism, blotted out the truth—the truth that I subconsciously craved from the depths of my soul.

Though I found the phenomenological perspective refreshing and perhaps even a little comforting for its protection of objective truth, I remained undecided on ethical theory. I didn't know if I should give my last bite of food to the young boy or the old man on the raft, or kill five strangers to save my one friend on the train tracks. The bottom line was, I was confused about the truth. And over time, I became more confused. What was once black and white to me as a child became a dull gray.

I needed a "lived theology"—a working biblical worldview I could apply in tough situations—if I wanted to make any sense of this world. Truth matters. If everything is about weighing pros and cons and just having the right heart, then what else could be justified? As I learned as a medical student and later as a doctor, this relative and proportional way of thinking persists in the halls of medical schools and hospitals, and it is used to justify the taking of countless human lives. If you can isolate Christ's truth from the difficult decisions you make every day, you can easily suffocate truth—and Christ *is* truth (Jn 14:6).

Outside of class, I thought little about God. I still prayed the Rosary once each week, but to me, it became a way to unwind after a long day—not a time to encounter God. I was too busy with schoolwork and baseball practice to participate in campus ministry or even go to Mass.

The tiniest dose of old-fashioned Catholic guilt would occasionally greet me around noon on Sundays when I'd roll out of bed after a late-night mixer on campus. I'd make my way toward the coffee shop and think briefly about my parish back home and whether or not Dad was playing the organ that morning. I'd picture Mom singing her favorite hymn, and for a moment I'd wish I were standing beside her. But the moment that first sip of piping hot coffee touched my lips, the guilt left me. I was free to go about the day with a clear conscience, because maybe I would catch the late evening Mass in the dorm.

But rarely did I go. If the priests say there are many ways to heaven and the Catholic Church teaches only one of the many ways, why bother attending Mass every week? If God understands our sin and that's all there is to it, then why bother confessing? If the leaders in the Church aren't teaching biblical truth on faith and morals, then why worry about whether or not I am walking in his ways? What I desired, but didn't even realize at the time, was the truth of a real, loving relationship with my Savior. But my commitment to God and his truth cooled until it became as lukewarm as a forgotten cup of coffee.

During my junior and senior years at Spring Hill College, I worked as a resident assistant for a co-ed freshman dorm on campus. I loved doing the weekend room checks because they were a social event for me. The other RAs would joke that it took me three times as long as the rest of them to check in with my students because I'd get caught up in conversation. The students would tell me about their classes and how stressed they were over exams and grades. The guys would share their drinking and girl stories. The girls would tell me about their hangovers and embarrassing moments from the night before. For whatever reason, the underclassmen trusted me.

Over time I developed strong relationships with the students in my dorm. Some of the girls came to me for dating advice when a guy wouldn't call them back. Others confided about issues at home or how they had decided to go on birth control behind their parents' backs. A few told me when they feared they were pregnant. They wanted someone to confide in and help them sort through the messiness of entering the college dating scene. The least I could do was listen attentively and share what wisdom I had. I became a communal older brother—someone who could offer secret insight into the male mind but also protect the women's interests when it came to relationships. Just as I had in high school, I enjoyed supporting my female friends this way and grew more in tune with the challenges women on campus faced when it came to dating and relationships.

One friend, who was dating one of my buddies on the baseball team, shared with me that she thought Christianity, and especially the Catholic Church, oppressed women, denying them their rights. In high school, I might have jumped to defend the Church, but as a college student, I considered myself more open-minded, so I asked her why she thought that way. Though she came from a Catholic family, she said she thought Church teaching on contraception, abortion, sexuality, and the role of women was outdated and that Vatican II should have gone further with its changes. She thought Catholics who still agreed with these positions were just hiding behind a "man-made" catechism and taking Bible verses out of context. It was absurd, she would argue, to assume King David was writing an anti-abortion song in Psalm 139 when he wrote, "You knitted me together in my mother's womb." She would proudly reel off facts she'd read in her sources, concluding that the question of when life begins is a matter for science to settle, not a single Bible verse. I listened without responding or agreeing, letting her words take up residence in my mind and my heart.

Many of my friends on campus agreed that the Church's position on these "women's issues" was generally patriarchal, especially when it came to contraception. A decade had passed since Pope Paul VI rejected contraception outright in his 1968 encyclical letter *Humanae vitae*, and many of my peers regarded his position as an outdated reinforcement of the domestic duties of motherhood.

John Paul II attempted to clarify the Church's understanding of women in his apostolic letters *On the Dignity of Women* (1988) and *Letter to Women* (1995). In these writings, he described the God-given "feminine genius" of all women while simultaneously opposing views of secular feminists regarding contraception, abortion, divorce, and the ordination of women. These writings came much later after the tumultuous upheaval of the two decades following Vatican II—too late for me and my peers to appreciate at Spring Hill College.

Confused by the seemingly conflicting messages from the Catholic Church, many of my friends' trust in Church teaching waned. More of them rejected Church doctrine on birth control and sexuality than accepted it. It seemed as though it was now permissible, and even *morally responsible*, to reject Church teachings and to follow one's conscience and personal convictions as the supreme moral compass.

I listened closely to my female peers in college about their opinions on feminism, abortion, contraception, and "outdated" Church teachings. Though I didn't form any strong opinions one way or the other—I was skilled at remaining lukewarm—I was willing to submit that they were probably right about a lot of these things. After all, they were women, and they would know better than I would about women's reproductive health. All I knew was that the feminist message sounded like a positive one, rooted in modern science. It was all about empowerment and equal rights and gaining control over their own body. Those all sounded like good things. Birth control prevents pregnancy in teens and women without the financial means to raise children. It frees women from the burdens of unwanted childbearing that would decrease their economic standing in society. I understood that contraception could reduce the number of abortions, though I agreed with my friends that abortion might be necessary in some cases, especially in cases of rape or when the mother's life is in danger. I believed that women should have the freedom to choose what is best for themselves.

Through these conversations with my peers, I learned something important about myself: I had a knack for listening to women and understanding the relational and reproductive challenges they faced even though I had no personal experience with these things as a man. Though I would not have attributed this mysterious gift to God at the time, he was beginning to form a passion for women's health in my heart. I thought back to the medical models I'd been so fascinated by as a boy, and I knew I wanted more than just to be a good listener and a trusted friend; I wanted to serve these women as their doctor, as someone who could really help them gain equality and control over their biology.

1982–1983

When the time came for me to apply to medical schools, Mom quickly volunteered to drive me up and down the East Coast for campus tours and interviews. She loved to travel and always kept an open suitcase at the foot of her bed. Though she suffered from chronic back pain and migraines most of her adult life, she had all the energy in the world if a long car trip was involved, especially if it meant spending time with one of her sons. Road tripping with Mom was always fun. She kept the conversation flowing, and when we weren't deep in discussion, she let me turn the radio up full blast and listen to whatever music I wanted.

It was a sunny April day in 1983 when Mom rushed up the front stairs and handed me a letter from the University of South Alabama College of Medicine. I gripped the envelope tight, closed my eyes, and said a quick prayer before tearing it open across the top. I'd received rejection letters from prestigious medical schools, and I was prepared for disappointment again. But this letter looked different. I didn't read past "We're pleased to inform you" before I threw my arms up in the air and Mom swooped in for a hug. I thanked God for the opportunity to pursue a career in medicine and to one day be his instrument for health and healing.

My cousin Rob, who had introduced me to the Visible Man and Woman models, called that afternoon to tell me he'd been accepted to medical school at East Carolina University. We celebrated over the phone and congratulated each other. After so many years of sharing this passion and dreaming of what could be, we were thrilled to begin our journeys to becoming good doctors together.

I wish I could say that I was, in fact, at that moment, on my way to becoming a good doctor. Armed with a growing base of medical knowledge and a proportionalist mindset of basing decisions on individual circumstances, I was confident in my own abilities as an aspiring doctor. But before I even started, I was firming up a bad habit of shutting God out of the operating room.

4

The First Time

I washed my hands with surgical scrub and antiseptic and slipped my arms through a sterile blue gown held up by a circulating nurse. Sliding my hands into tight surgical gloves, I walked into Dr. Cohen's operating room at the University of South Alabama Hospital. A woman sat silently on the exam table, covered in blue medical drapes from the waist down. I had reviewed her medical chart while she was in the presurgical waiting area. She was just over 40 years old, a mother of three, and pregnant with her fourth by surprise. Today's procedure: elective abortion. She had said that she couldn't support another child and asked Dr. Cohen to "take care of it" for her.

The anesthesiologist stood silently at his work station at the head of the patient's bed, waiting for his cue. In the presurgical area, the patient had already received an oral cocktail of medications, including Valium to quiet her anxiety and an antacid to calm her stomach. The anesthesiologist studied the neatly arranged syringes on his cart. We spoke in hushed tones as he administered oxygen and anesthesia and Dr. Cohen checked his instruments.

The OB/GYN department at the University of South Alabama Hospital didn't usually refer pregnant women for abortions, but this woman was Dr. Cohen's patient from his private practice. The hospital staff supported Dr. Cohen in the operating room whenever he performed procedures on his own patients, and they acted with the utmost discretion when the procedure was an abortion. The chart outside the door of the operating room would be marked with the letters "VIP", which did not mean "very important person", but "voluntary interruption of pregnancy".

Silence veiled the room, as if we could hide what we were about to do. I knew somewhere deep down that what we were "interrupting" was a human life. Within a matter of minutes, I would stop the beating heart of an unborn child. But as quickly as these rushing thoughts invaded my mind, threatening my involvement in the procedure, I blocked them out. Instead, I focused my attention on the intricate steps I would perform to complete the dilation and curettage. Dr. Cohen leaned into my shoulder and whispered, "You can step in now, if you want."

My heart began to pound. I was a third-year medical student, and this would be my first elective abortion. I turned my attention to my breath, a familiar habit I had formed to focus while throwing relief pitches in college. I suppressed the sudden urge to run and exhaled slowly, releasing the breath from my pursed lips so no one could sense my mounting anxiety.

It was the first time Dr. Cohen had asked me to join him in the operating room. Usually students were randomly assigned to shadow a particular surgeon, but Dr. Cohen had sought me out for this procedure, and I knew it was a big deal that he was allowing me to help. He was my favorite professor and mentor, and also a well-published attending doctor whom I deeply respected. Many of my classmates had hoped for such an opportunity, and I felt privileged to work so closely with him that morning. Dr. Cohen had given me the choice whether or not to step in because he knew about my Catholic background and didn't want to pressure me into participating in anything that made me uncomfortable. But he also knew I was interested in obstetrics and gynecology and eager to soak up as much knowledge and experience as I could.

Part of me didn't want to be there. I had never participated in an elective abortion before, let alone performed one, and I was still not quite sure how I felt about the procedure. At 10 weeks' gestational age, the fetus, I knew, had a heart that had been beating for at least 5 weeks already, sending its own blood to all of its organs, which were already in place and beginning to function in purposeful development. But I feared turning Dr. Cohen's offer down would make me look like a bad medical student, especially after the personal invitation to assist him. The last thing I wanted was for this respected physician and personal mentor to think I wasn't fully invested and eager to take advantage of opportunities to learn. I reasoned that I probably had no choice but to perform these procedures if I ever wanted to go into OB/GYN, so I would follow his lead and get over my uncertainty. I'd see how I felt afterward and decide then whether or not I'd do it again.

Nervous that I had already revealed too much hesitancy, I quickly accepted and waited for his direction. He gestured toward the surgical stool and asked me to examine the patient's uterus before surgery. As the adrenaline coursed through my veins, I again reminded myself to breathe. Nurses prepped and draped the patient, placing her thighs in padded stirrups as we washed and gowned. Next, I performed a pelvic exam to better understand the size and position of her uterus, which would help us determine how deep and in which orientation to place the instruments during the procedure. I reported my findings to Dr. Cohen, and he confirmed my description.

We were performing a standard dilation and curettage to remove the child from the patient's uterus. It was a procedure I had performed on women before, but only after the fetus had miscarried and the cervix had naturally softened to begin the process of expelling the dead fetus. This was the first time I'd been called in to assist with a dilation and curettage on a woman with an *unwanted* pregnancy, whose baby was still alive. I knew it would be a much different experience from a miscarriage, both for her and for me. In the case of the miscarriage, the body is getting ready to expel the dead child. In this case, the body would hold on to the baby.

After the speculum was in place, Dr. Cohen paused to give me a few important reminders for the procedure. "Don't worry about bleeding," he instructed. "Move quickly, but thoroughly. Suction in a circular motion: twelve o'clock, three o'clock, six o'clock, nine, then back to twelve."

Together Dr. Cohen and I grasped the top half of the patient's cervix with a sharp-toothed tenaculum clamp. Next, I slowly slid a thin dilating rod through the vaginal opening to begin dilating her cervix. I repeated this step with the next metal rod from the row on the table beside me, each slightly wider than the last: 3 millimeters, then 4 millimeters, then 5 millimeters, until the diameter of her cervix measured 12 millimeters, just wide enough to extract a 10-week-old fetus. Dr. Cohen checked her progress and handed me the suction cannula—a rigid, bent, hollow tube 9.5 inches in length.

With his hand on my wrist, he guided me, sliding the cannula through her cervix and into her uterus. Once it was in place, he attached the suction tubing and turned on the machine to begin the extraction. The machine hummed as it revved up to the appropriate pressure level in the green zone of the dial. It was time to begin the curettage. We rhythmically moved the suction cannula in and out and all around the uterine cavity to sweep the entire space where the fetus and placenta were growing.

I felt a tiny jolt in my hands and watched as tissue entered the cannula and rushed along the clear tubing into a graduated canister on the table behind me. Some of the tissue passing through the cannula appeared gray and white; other pieces were pink and red. After Dr. Cohen believed we had extracted as much of the fetus and placenta as we could with the suction cannula, we gently removed it and cleared the small bits of remaining tissue in the uterine cavity with polyp forceps. We finished by scraping her entire uterine cavity with a curette to make sure nothing was left behind.

The humming of the suction machine stopped, and silence fell over the operating room for a moment. I removed the tenaculum clamp that was holding the cervix in place. A brief stream of blood began to flow as the pressure from the clamp was released. I observed until it stopped. In the final step of the procedure, I removed the speculum, placed it on the table beside me, and stood up to blot the beads of sweat that had accumulated above my brow before anyone noticed. As the woman came out of anesthesia, a nurse lifted her legs out of the stirrups, transferred her to a gurney, and wheeled her to a recovery room.

We had completed a VIP—a voluntary interruption of pregnancy—one of the most commonly performed surgical procedures in the world. I did it, and I survived. But instead of the sense of satisfaction that I usually felt after performing a procedure, I felt a kind of gnawing absence that I couldn't quite understand or articulate. I wondered if the patient felt what I felt, since we were connected by this procedure. If she did, would relief ever replace her feeling of loss?

Dr. Cohen and I turned our attention to the canister on the table behind us. Dr. Cohen lifted the lid and disconnected the tubing, exposing a mesh bag, which separated fetal tissue from the blood and amniotic fluids collected during the procedure. He pointed out the amount of blood lost in the procedure: normal. Then, unfurling the tissue bag, he fingered small pieces of fetal tissue—four tiny limbs, abdominal organs, and the parts of a fractured head. "Yep, looks about right for 10 weeks' gestation," he confirmed.

It was a grotesque process necessary to ensure that no fetal tissue was left inside the woman's uterus, which could cause heavy bleeding, infection, and in rare cases, death. He closed up the mesh bag, sealed it in a red biohazardous waste bag, and tossed it in a biohazard trash can. "You did well, John," he said, turning to me. "You can head out now. I'll handle the paperwork."

I thought I'd feel at least a twinge of remorse after participating in the procedure with Dr. Cohen. But I didn't feel much of anything at all. Going into it, I had wondered if I could follow through with the procedure once I started, if I'd feel guilty, not wanting to look cowardly in front of my professor. But, as it turned out, the few extra steps required to open the tightly sealed cervix didn't change much about how I thought about the procedure. Once I got beyond that, it felt no different from the procedures I'd performed on women who needed our help after their pregnancies ended in miscarriage. *It just wasn't a big deal*, I told myself, ignoring the obvious differences. *Just another dilation and curettage like I've done many times before, and after today, will likely do many more times.*

Luckily for me, the busy pace of medical school distracted me from thinking about the abortion much after that day. But when the occasional thought did seep into my mind that I had, in fact, done something horrible, I'd push it out by reminding myself that the abortion would have happened whether or not my hand had been on the cannula with Dr. Cohen's. I wasn't the one making the call—the burden of responsibility fell on the patient and Dr. Cohen. Not me. Plus, we were taught to trust our patients above all else, and for whatever reason, this woman felt the abortion would make life better for her. It wasn't my place to question her choices. I was there to help women, to make my patients happy, and to earn a reputation as a trusted and caring physician. If an abortion was a woman's desire, I would provide that service to the best of my ability to the women in my care.

1983–1986

During my four years at the University of South Alabama Medical College, I devoted myself to learning as much as I possibly could. When I wasn't in the classroom or the lab, I spent what felt like every waking hour memorizing the minutiae of biochemical processes, the names and innervations of nerves, the disbursement of oxygen through the tiniest blood vessels, and the mysterious synaptic processes in the brain. Wide-eyed and scribbling notes, I listened to lectures, totally enthralled with all of it.

In my physiology and biochemistry classes at South Alabama, I was overwhelmed with wonder at the design of the body. The formation and replication of DNA strands astounded me—the way they gracefully wrap around themselves in spiraling declarations of the uniqueness of life. The way trillions of microscopic cells come together to create functioning organs, each with its own specific purpose. The synchronization of millions of systems, from the tiniest cell division to the massive complexity of the digestive system, all working together to create one rhythmic pattern of life. I saw an intentional order to the human body, and, therefore, to the whole person.

But when it came time to start clinical rounds in my third year, I found that I enjoyed interacting with patients far more than the didactic book learning I had experienced in the classroom during my first two years. My heart came alive in the exam room, where I could apply all the incredible knowledge I had collected to the person sitting on the table before me. Each day I went into the clinic, I sensed that I was finally fulfilling the desire God had planted in my heart so many years before, following the path my cousin Rob and I had dreamt about together for so long.

I quickly formed strong relationships with several of my professors, who mentored me and taught me how to make logical diagnostic and therapeutic decisions in both the clinic and the operating room. I deeply valued my professors and worked hard to earn their approval, because I wanted them to see my commitment to being an excellent physician.

Dr. Cohen was hands down my most influential mentor. A Jewish man raised in New Jersey and educated in New York, he teased me relentlessly about my Polish roots and how I was becoming "too southern". Nonetheless, his New Jersey accent made me feel right at home in the Deep South, and we bonded over our similar upbringings and our shared interest in obstetrics and gynecology. As an OB/GYN, Dr. Cohen specialized in hematologic diseases in pregnancy, which in Mobile meant he became an expert in treating African American women suffering from sickle cell disease. He was a brilliant and tenderhearted man who took the time to listen to his patients and his residents. He and another mentor, Dr. Sorello, spoke highly of me among their peers and together were responsible for convincing me that I was good enough to become an OB/GYN. More than the other professional mentors in my life, Dr. Cohen became a mentor-friend, one whose professional advice had a profound impact in my heart.

I sympathized with Dr. Cohen's position on abortion: that abortion should be a safe and shame-free standard of care available to any woman for any reason she felt was sufficient. Above all, she should be trusted to make the best decision for herself, and a good doctor would support her without question or doubt. This position was considered "best practice" in the field of obstetrics in the 1980s, and I was willing to accept the mainstream teaching. I was also heavily influenced by some of my peers in school, who believed abortion was compassionate medicine for women facing poverty or strained relationships, or feeling too overwhelmed to bring a child into the world. Through experience in performing a handful of abortions with Dr. Cohen and listening to the stories of our patients who felt that abortion was their only option, my heart began to sink deeper into the ideology that surrounded me. The issue of abortion became one I was comfortable categorizing as a moral gray zone, in which one must simply weigh the pros and cons of each unique situation and make the best decision. Coupled with a misguided compassion for my female patients in medical school, I began to view abortion as an acceptable, even compassionate, form of medical treatment.

I did not appreciate how quickly the darkness was overtaking me, as if I were wearing rose-colored sunglasses at dusk. Almost without my noticing it, I began to pray less, and my church attendance waned. In the years that followed, my heart would continue to harden on the abortion issue, and eventually I came to believe that abortion was justifiable for nearly any reason, at any time, at any stage of development. The medical treatment evolved in my mind from a necessary evil to *good* medicine.

1985–1986

During my third year of medical school, I was assigned to the health department in the hospital in downtown Mobile for what would become my favorite clerkship rotation. The health department offered obstetrical care and also free birth control to low-income patients—a service I was passionate about providing. Many of our patients were single mothers, often with several young children at home, trying to survive on welfare. With few opportunities and the too-costly expense of full-time childcare, most didn't have jobs or a committed partner with a job. Most couldn't afford birth control on their own.

In a world of poverty, childbearing did not seem to be the blessing that I had always thought it to be and that most people made it out to be. I was beginning to see that in the dire circumstances of inner-city poverty, bearing children was a chore and raising them a financial burden, on both the mother and the taxpayers. I pitied the pregnant women who came into our clinic wondering how they would raise the children in their wombs and what quality of life those children would have growing up in the rougher neighborhoods of our city, where opportunities didn't come around very often and crime seemed to lure young people with a magnetic force. Providing free birth control felt like an act of mercy, a way to help these

women and their families rise above the difficult circumstances in their lives.

At the Mobile clinic, I was primarily responsible for
inserting intrauterine devices (IUDs) for my patients. Many
of the women I saw were diabetic, which precluded birth
control pills as an option for them, since the added estrogen would interfere with their bodies' ability to process
insulin. Others were just sick of taking a pill every day and
thrilled to have a lower-maintenance birth control option.
I'd explain that I would first numb their cervix to ease the
pain, and then they'd feel a slight twinge after the IUD
was placed. I'd warn of strong cramping during and after
the procedure, which would fade after a few days, and of
the small possibility of infection and the even-smaller possibility of perforation of the uterus. I can't recall one of my
patients ever hesitating. They cheerfully gave the green
light, thrilled to have an easy contraception option that
nearly guaranteed that they didn't have to worry about any
unwanted pregnancies.

I felt as if I were making a positive difference in the lives
of these women by empowering them through access to
birth control and working to make abortions, when necessary, the safe standard of care. I was thrilled to work at a
clinic that helped the underserved and taught them good
stewardship of their fertility.

But not all my colleagues thought about our patients the
same way. Some of the women would come to appointments with three or four other children in tow. Knowing that many of these women were unemployed single
mothers without committed partners, my colleagues occasionally whispered judgmental comments in passing. "*She*
could use an IUD," they'd mutter, suggesting the mother
had made a poor choice by not using birth control sooner.
Whenever my colleagues mocked our patients in private

like this, I made a point to withhold any nods of agreement or affirming chuckles. I didn't like their questioning of our patients' personal choices or assuming the children were not entirely wanted in the first place. After all, shouldn't they have just as much of a right to *have* children as to prevent becoming pregnant?

The patients were my favorite part of working at the clinic in Mobile. I enjoyed talking and laughing with them and often stepped out of the office to see one or two straggling behind to chat or crack another joke with me before leaving the clinic. One of my patients was so comfortable with me that she teased me about my boyish looks and sparse facial hair. "Boy, if you're going to be between the legs of a mature woman, you had better grow a beard and look a little older and wiser!" I had kept clean-shaven in medical school, but after her teasing, I quit shaving and never looked back.

In the context of the sometimes-awkward nature of gynecological care, both my patients and I enjoyed the friendly banter and jokes at my expense. The deep trust that developed between patient and doctor in these light-hearted conversations was especially helpful before procedures that at times were somewhat uncomfortable or painful. In the end, the women knew I cared about them, and they trusted that I would take good care of them.

One evening in the hallway at the University of South Alabama Hospital, Dr. Cohen pulled me aside and asked, "John, do you have a quick minute to grab dinner after I see this patient?"

I rarely passed up an opportunity to learn from Dr. Cohen. We often discussed what type of medicine I'd like to pursue after medical school, whether I should go into emergency medicine, family medicine, or obstetrics and gynecology. Dr. Cohen had a vested interest in guiding me to the right choice, and now that it was time to start thinking about residencies, I was hoping he'd have some helpful advice to share with me. I met him downstairs shortly after. Though my conversations with Dr. Cohen were always positive, I couldn't help but feel a bit nervous whenever I met with an attending doctor.

"John, I know you've been thinking about a few options for your residency, but I want to tell you that I've been thinking about it a lot, and I see a future for you in obstetrics. You really have what it takes to be a good OB/GYN."

With relief, I thanked him, though it was difficult to accept such a compliment from one of my heroes.

"I really mean it. You know, you scored super high on the end-of-rotation exam. You're smart, you have the technical chops, and you know how to make wise clinical decisions. But you're also a thoughtful listener, and I can tell the patients really connect with you. They really love having you as their clinic doctor."

His validation was just what I wanted to hear, especially that he saw patients enjoying my company. I didn't just want to be a smart doctor; I wanted to be a doctor who could empathize and connect with his patients on a personal level, and his compliment was the best I'd hoped to receive. "Wow. Thanks, Dr. Cohen. You know, I've loved learning from you, and this clerkship has made me seriously consider becoming an OB/GYN one day. I've been trying to decide if delivering babies is what I'm meant to do." I took another bite of my cheeseburger, thankful that Dr. Cohen had noticed my gifts and talents. The cafeteria burgers were never very good, but after working a 12-hour shift and feeling validated in my hard work, this one tasted much more satisfying than it should have.

Things were starting to fall into place, and my career path seemed to be laid out before me. I was beginning to see a clear direction for the future, and I wondered if I had just uncovered my life's calling.

"John, if you do decide to go into obstetrics and gynecology, you can make a great living. Especially if you offer *all* the pregnancy services for women."

I nodded, understanding that he was referring to abortions. Dr. Cohen had always tread lightly when discussing abortion with me out of sensitivity for my Catholic upbringing. Now he wasn't sure how I felt about making elective abortions part of my future career. And, frankly, neither was I.

Pushing his empty plate aside, Dr. Cohen clasped his hands on the table in front of him and leaned in close. "John, offering abortions would double or even triple your income and earn you respect in the field. Health care is changing, and this is a service that's going to be standard practice in every OB/GYN clinic in the country. It's just a fact that you need to consider, that's all."

Though money was never the biggest motivator for me, I nodded in agreement and told him I understood that surgery was where the money was in gynecology.

As we left the hospital cafeteria, going our separate ways, I replayed the conversation in my head. I knew I could make a decent living as a doctor, but double or triple what I had imagined sure was appealing, especially considering the student loan payments I'd be faced with in a few years. In medical school, I'd taken care of Dr. Cohen's beautiful home on the river when he was out of town, and I knew I could enjoy similar luxuries if I followed in his footsteps. Plus, my parents were starting to get older now, and I wanted to make sure I could provide for them when the time came. Of course, no one *wants* to do abortions, but I had seen firsthand circumstances that seemed to justify them. If I truly cared about women and what they wanted, if I really wanted to help women get out of poverty and pursue better lives for themselves and their families, shouldn't I be willing to perform abortions in extreme cases? Thinking back on my anatomy models, I realized that I had been interested in women's health for a very long time. As I wandered through the hospital halls and back to my rotational work, it became clear to me: I was going into obstetrics and gynecology.

1987—Virginia

My externship in rural Virginia further confirmed my decision to become an OB/GYN. Though I worked at an internal medicine clinic and not an obstetrics or gynecology practice, it was there that I met two heroic physicians whom I wanted to emulate. Through their friendships, I was influenced by their thinking on women's health, but most of all, I was inspired by the genuine love they showed their patients and the community.

Serving low-income women in Mobile had given me a passion for helping people in my own community, but the Jesuit model at my undergraduate college taught me to focus on the "underserved", meaning people in places *other* than where I lived. At the time, good friends of mine were traveling to faraway places like Guatemala and Tibet on mission trips and international rotations for medical school. Their stories all sounded so exciting, but I had seen firsthand that there were plenty of poor and underserved people right here at home, in the wealthiest country in the world. Since I had gained good experience with inner-city medicine in Mobile, I wanted to understand the health challenges that faced rural populations and the medical interventions most necessary for them. Near the end of my fourth and final year of medical school, I left the South for a tiny health clinic in the heart of Appalachia in the southwestern tip of Virginia.

The clinic I was assigned to was in a small former coal-mining town nestled in the mountains just north of the Kentucky border. The town's neighboring communities saw some of their hardest times when the coal wars of the 1930s broke out over poor mining conditions and wages. Despite the surrounding clashes, this town saw its hey-day in the 1930s and 1940s when coal mining was most profitable in the region. Employment was seldom lacking, houses were popping up everywhere, and this hardwork-ing community thrived with opportunity. But when the coal industry began to decline, the same companies that had infused life into this small town packed up their profits in search of the next big thing.

The population hovered between 200 and 250 in the 1980s and has been dropping ever since. In search of bet-ter access to health care and nearby groceries, those with means left for the big cities: Johnson City, Tennessee; Richmond, Virginia; and Charlotte, North Carolina. Many young people who stayed ended up spending their time on the street corner after the coal company shut its doors and moved on. Nearly half of the people who stayed in the town lived below the poverty line, which in 1985 hovered just over $10,000 for a family of four. Those lucky enough to hold steady jobs, no matter how meager the income, were grateful not to be counted among the ranks of the unemployed. Still, the locals took pride in their community and worked hard to keep it alive.

Today, a mural is proudly displayed on the side of a church building depicting the town as a field of emerald grass with a creek running from the softly curved moun-tains in the distance. Painted over the grassy meadows are

the words "The City of the Lord". The mural is a lovely
welcome to the small town, but in the mid-1980s, this
place felt like anything but God's city.

When I arrived, empty houses and storefronts, once
jam-packed with life and energy, lined the main street
with boarded up windows and "For Sale" signs. The opera
house hadn't been used in over 20 years. A post office, an
elementary school, and a few churches were the only signs
of life. The houses on the outskirts were simple, with shacks
in the valley or "the holler", some with heavy old rugs in
place of doors. The roads were ancient and pot-holed. Dark
dust and grime muted the vibrant colors of nature, stuck
mercilessly to your skin, and brought a gray lifelessness to
the air. The Appalachian Mountains sloped behind a town
defeated by the coal industry and holding on to a hollow
hope that mining jobs would come back one day.

Serving the former coal town and the surrounding areas
was a health clinic, a one-story building with a humble
waiting room, several exam rooms, and two offices: one
for a young physician assistant from Yale, Katrina Early,
and one for Dr. De Vries.

Katrina had grown up in the suburbs of Detroit. Her
parents had been deeply affected by the oppression their
own Jewish families had faced, and they stressed the inher-
ent dignity of all people as they stood up in support of
the oppressed and marginalized, marching with Dr. Mar-
tin Luther King to campaign for African American voting
rights in the 1960s. Like her family members before her,
Katrina was on a mission to make the world around her a
better place. After graduating as a physician's assistant from
Yale, Katrina moved to southwestern Virginia to serve the
rural communities of Appalachia. She lived among the
people whom she served, bringing joy and dignity to those
around her.

Leading the health clinic as head physician was Dr. De Vries, an out-of-towner who had made the community his home. Like Katrina, he had moved to rural Appalachia immediately after he graduated as valedictorian of his medical school and residency, turning down lucrative offers in much more comfortable parts of the country and choosing instead to care for the medically underserved of the region. Dr. De Vries was a great doctor—well-read, thorough, thoughtful, a good listener, and always on call. He was a self-proclaimed communist and fervently committed to the politics of the region, so much so that when the water spouts poured out black sludge because the streams were backed up with coal pollution, he spoke publicly against the injustices of the coal companies to the Environmental Protection Agency. He used his knowledge of the people and his status as a physician to speak out for the betterment of the town he loved. The locals loved and respected Dr. De Vries so much that when he and his wife, Sarah, were married, half the town came to his wedding. Towering over most of us with his slender six-foot-four-inch frame, he dressed in simple clothes, consumed only according to his basic needs, and lived his convictions to the fullest.

Together, Dr. De Vries and Katrina offered basic family care to men and women in the community. They treated patients suffering from coal-induced black lung disease, diabetes, and common colds. Both worked long hours and knew their patients on a personal level. Dr. De Vries often spoke with his patients about their struggles with depression and economic hardships and their concerns about living with chronic lung diseases. When women opened up to Katrina about their absent, unemployed, alcoholic husbands, she always lent an attentive ear. Though patients rarely complied with her basic health instructions, ignored referrals for drug and alcohol rehabilitation, and expressed an overall distrust in medical professionals, Dr. De Vries and Katrina never gave up on them. The government, Jesus, and history had all forgotten them, they'd say, but these doctors hadn't. I pledged not to either.

Even for the short six weeks I was there, I strove to immerse myself in the community as much as possible and learn more about the holler lifestyle. I was careful not to rush patients I treated, and I let them speak freely about their days. I learned that violent family brawls were common and that some neighbors used weapons against one another to defend their honor when needed. I got a taste of the town feuds when a gang of unemployed men slashed all of my tires the week I moved there. Perhaps they wanted to let me know they weren't pleased that a Yankee with a Jersey accent had moved to their town. Maybe the slashing was the reckless destruction of a drunken dare, misplaced anger over their unemployment, or just plain boredom. Whatever the reason, it certainly wasn't the challenge I had expected to find in my first week of rotation. But, as it turned out, a few of their girlfriends were patients at the clinic and must have put in a good word for me, because just days later, the men returned to replace my slashed tires with four new ones.

When it came time to bring children into the world, the local women wanted to deliver in their homes, not in hospitals. I assisted in one delivery out in the holler but spent most of my time treating patients for general medical problems at the clinic, making house calls for blood draws, and shadowing Dr. De Vries at the hospital outside of town. But it was through the time spent in conversation with Dr. De Vries and Katrina, between patients or during quick lunch breaks, that the conviction that medicine should be used to serve my fellow man began to take root deeply in my heart.

Knowing I was interested in pursuing an OB/GYN specialty, Dr. De Vries and Katrina shared their perspectives on contraception and abortion and the role these services played in poor rural towns. They were both avid believers in the "my body, my choice" approach to women's health. Dr. De Vries shared stories of women they knew who had eight, nine, or ten children and the unnecessary hardships they faced simply because they didn't have access to free contraception. In his opinion, unplanned children were a direct road to poverty in this town, if you weren't already below the poverty line. That's why he offered to write prescriptions for birth control pills for his female patients and referred some of them to abortion facilities. Knowing about my Catholic upbringing, he would gently remind me about the need for these services, saying things like, "You know, John, in this day and age the woman's right to choose is very important." And I would assure him I was already making my peace with the changing demands of health care in general, and OB/GYN in particular.

It seemed that the most caring physicians in my life supported modern feminism and a woman's right to choose abortion: Dr. Cohen, and now Dr. De Vries and Katrina. I wanted to be a caring practitioner like them. I admired their convictions and the way they heroically lived them out by showing true compassion for the people in their community. By the end of my time in Appalachia, I knew in my heart that I wanted to be an OB/GYN who was proud to provide women the treatments they needed to get out of poverty, to free them from the chains of their fertility, and to offer them a chance at a better life.

One afternoon, I was making house calls with a local volunteer named Becca who helped us navigate the terrain. Since many of the houses out in the holler were unmarked and invisible from the road, we depended on

Becca's help in finding the homes of some of the most medically vulnerable residents. As we walked toward the town discussing our patient list for the day, Becca turned to me with a pointed question. "Do you plan to stay here after you graduate?"

"No," I told her, "I'm only here for a few weeks for an elective in rural medicine to help underserved populations."

Her eyes squinted in disapproval, and I immediately regretted my choice of words. "So, you're just like the rest who come, then—you see us as poor and needy."

I felt my eyebrows rise in shock, but I let her continue.

"You come here to check off the box and clean your conscience and then you leave for bigger and better things. You ain't giving back. You're just using us to make yourself feel good, like everybody else does." Anger filled her eyes and her voice. "We *are* somebody. Why does everyone forget about us? The government forgot us. The church forgot us. The coal company used us, spit us out, poisoned our people and left us, too. All we get is promises with no follow-through. You're just like the rest of 'em."

I'd never heard her talk this way before. Her words kicked me square in the gut, and I knew she was right. What good was practicing here for such a short period of time? I had learned what I wanted to about rural medicine, but what good had I really done for the people here? I'd diagnosed and treated patients, sure, and I'd helped relieve Dr. De Vries of some of his patient load. But any medical student could have done that. I wanted to make a real difference in people's lives, and until this point, I had thought I was doing a pretty good job. But what good would I be as a doctor if I went back to the promise of a comfortable life with no intention of remembering the poor, of remembering Becca and her rightful anger? We finished the rounds that day in silence.

Some of the great women I had learned about growing up—Mother Teresa, Catherine Doherty, Dorothy Day—all lived in the communities in which they served, just like Katrina and Dr. De Vries. They lived there, worked there, served there, and became family to the people in their cities. They cared about the issues that affected those they served, because they were equally affected as their neighbors, peers, and friends. But I was not living up to the example they set. I had come to this small town because I thought staying in the United States was a more noble and authentic choice than going overseas. But in the end, I would leave rural Appalachia just as my peers would leave Guatemala and Tibet: with few lasting patient relationships and no lasting impact. And that's all my patients had been to me: patients. I hadn't seen them as neighbors, as peers, as family. Indeed, I had forgotten them. And in a very real sense, I had never really known them.

5

Guadalupe

1987

Back in Mobile, I prepared dinner with my roommate Gabe and our close friend Paul. In the last weeks of medical school, after having just accepted a prestigious residency with Eastern Virginia Medical School at Norfolk General Hospital in Virginia, I had more time for casual dinners and social events.

Gabe was a good friend from college and a faithful Catholic. He introduced me to Paul, whom he knew from church, during my first year in Mobile, and the three of us had been nearly inseparable ever since. Neither Gabe nor Paul was in medical school, which allowed me the sanity of hanging around nonmedical folks sometimes and talking about nonmedical things. Paul was interested in history, as I was, and we shared many evenings in our living room with Gabe, drinking beer and having lively discussions.

As far as I knew, Paul was also the only evangelical Christian in the entire state of Alabama who'd converted to Catholicism. Catholics became Baptists down there, not the other way around. I had always respected Paul's independent thinking, his love for Christ, and his devotion to Mary. He had a way of refocusing my attention on the faith of my childhood by his living example and through conversations about Scripture. One night, we found ourselves deep in discussion about the book of Revelation, and he suggested we read it aloud together, straight through, from beginning to end. When we finished reading, he posed a question for us to think about: "Do we live as if eternity matters?"

I stopped to think about this one. *Do I?* We talked long into the night as he fired off thought-provoking questions about Jesus and who we believed him to be. Though I found our discussions and his questions interesting, I wasn't independently devoted to studying Scripture. I simply enjoyed intellectual conversations like these with Paul and was happy to go along with them, though his fierce reliance on God had a way of reminding me that my own faith had grown stale.

This particular night, Gabe set all the taco fixings on the table, and Paul cracked open cold beers for us. No sooner had we all taken our seats than Paul proposed an adventure that Gabe and I couldn't refuse. "My priest friend in Mexico City called me today. He needs help building a water purifying system for his parishioners in their neighborhood and asked me if I would fly down and help him build it."

"Oh yeah? Are you going?" I asked.

"Yes, I think so. But I was wondering if y'all would want to come with me. Father Mike needs all the extra hands he can get."

I rarely turned down a chance to travel to another state or country for an adventure, something I got from Mom. "Sure! I'd love to go." Not to be left out, Gabe quickly accepted the invitation as well, and we got busy discussing all the details.

The five-day trip would be a much-needed break before the stressful transition to my residency in Virginia.

My experience in the Deep South had been a rewarding one, but I was looking forward to a change of scenery and living closer to my family in New Jersey. Plus, I was on a social justice kick after working in rural medicine in Appalachia, and I was eager for another opportunity to help a community in need.

I was also interested in visiting the famous Basilica of Our Lady of Guadalupe that my parents had told me about when I was a young boy. Located near Mexico City, the church displays a famous Catholic relic, an over-450-year-old cloak featuring an image of the Virgin Mary. Before we left for Mexico, I refreshed my memory on the story of Juan Diego, the original owner of the cloak displayed at the Basilica. Born in 1474, Juan Diego had witnessed human sacrifices under Aztec rule, until the Spanish conquistadors invaded Mexico, overthrowing Aztec power and introducing Roman Catholicism to the region in the early 1520s. Juan Diego and his wife were among the first converts of the Aztec people, and Juan Diego quickly became a devout Catholic. Six years later, on December 9, 1531, Juan Diego was on his way to morning Mass when a beautiful maiden appeared to him as he passed Tepeyac Hill. The woman was dressed like an Aztec princess and spoke to Juan Diego in his native language, but she also wore a cross at her neck, the symbol of the Spanish conquistadors. She wore a sash around her waist, which was the traditional Aztec garment worn by women who were with child. She identified herself as the Virgin Mary and instructed Juan Diego to tell the bishop to construct a shrine in her honor on Tepeyac Hill.

The Spanish bishop, skeptical about the unlikely story of an Aztec convert, told Juan Diego to ask the woman for a sign. In the meantime, Juan Diego's uncle had fallen gravely ill. On December 12, he went in search of a priest to perform the Last Rites for his dying uncle. The Virgin Mary intercepted his route and gently scolded Juan Diego for not trusting in her love, saying to him, "nothing whatever should frighten you or worry you.... do not fear ... illness or calamity. Am I, your mother, not here?"[1] She assured Juan Diego that his uncle had been cured. She also told Juan Diego to gather roses from the top of the hill as the sign for the bishop, an unlikely find in the frosty December ground. In obedience, he gathered roses and delivered them to the bishop that same day.

When Juan Diego opened his *tilma*, or cloak, before the bishop, the roses fell to the floor, revealing that sacred image of Our Lady of Guadalupe on the fabric. Today, Juan Diego's tilma is not only a religious treasure, but a symbol of Mexican nationalism, as the woman equally embodies indigenous and European cultures.

Though it is a fascinating and inspiring story, I questioned its historical validity and wrote off the appearance of Our Lady of Guadalupe as a Catholic myth. Such a detailed image of the Virgin Mary appearing on a poncho woven with cactus fibers seemed like a pretty far-fetched claim to me. *Juan Diego likely did it himself*, I reasoned. The famous tilma was probably a fraud.

Still, there was no doubt the story had shaped Mexico and its people for centuries. As we know from our own country's dark chapters of history, the Europeans did not treat the natives well, to say the least. The Virgin Mary's resemblance to an Aztec princess seemed to demonstrate her love for the indigenous people and the poor. The Aztecs had a violent ritual of offering human

---

[1] Luis Lasa de la Vega, *The Story of Guadalupe, Luis Lasa de la Vega's* Huei tlamahuiçoltica *of 1649*, trans. and ed. Lisa Sousa, Stafford Poole, C.M., and James Lockhart (Stanford, California: Stanford University Press, 1998), 77–79.

sacrifices, many of them children, to their own gods. Some historians claim that over 50,000 people fell victim to the human sacrifice practice every year, and one in every five children was killed.[2] With the conquest of the oppressive Aztec regime and the end of human sacrifice in the region, 9,000,000 Aztecs embraced the Catholic faith, and peace spread through Mexico.[3] And if peace in such a violent land was the result of a calculated myth, I figured that was at least a pretty good outcome.

It was certainly an interesting story, but I was admittedly more excited to eat Mexican street food and drink *cervezas* with Paul and Gabe than I was to reconnect with my faith in Mexico. Still, I knew traveling with two pious Catholics and staying with a priest probably meant we'd attend daily Mass, and I'd probably spend a good deal of time looking up at that inexplicable poncho.

Just a few weeks later, we jetted off to Mexico City and stayed with Father Mike, a tall blond-haired and blue-eyed priest known as "Padre" in his neighborhood. He greeted us warmly when we arrived, offered us tortillas and cheese for a late dinner, and showed us to our rooms.

We spent our first full day working on the water purification system for the parishioners at the church: laying a foundation, redirecting the flow of water into the system, and moving any cinder blocks we could find to form a wall around the newly installed purifier. Father Mike was pleasantly surprised by the turnout of local men

[2] Warren H. Carroll, "Honoring Christopher Columbus", *Faith & Reason* 18, no. 2 (Summer 1992), https://media.christendom.edu/1992/06/honoring -christopher-columbus/.

[3] "God Intervened through Our Lady of Guadalupe to Evangelize the Americas, Explains Guadalupe Expert", *Catholic News Agency*, August 11, 2009, https://www.catholicnewsagency.com/news/god_intervened_through_our _lady_of_guadalupe_to_evangelize_the_americas_explains_guadalupe_expert.

who volunteered to help us, and I enjoyed getting to work hard beside them for the health and betterment of their city.

The next day, Father Mike drove us to visit Aztec temples and pyramids in and around the city, where human sacrifices had been performed centuries before. In the most commonly performed ritual, the sacrifice—usually men, but occasionally children[4]—would be escorted to the top of the temple and laid on a stone slab. A priest would then slice open the chest of the living victim and extract the heart.[5] The priest would hold the beating heart toward the sky to honor the sun god, Huitzilopochtli, and the body would be tossed down the pyramid stairs.[6] Imagining a culture centered around violent human slaughter left me with a queasy feeling in my stomach.

Later that day, we took the metro to the north side of the city to visit the Basilica of Our Lady of Guadalupe, the church that displays Saint Juan Diego's famous tilma. It was extremely hot and humid summer day, sunnier and steamier than usual for high desert. Even on a weekday, the metro was packed with Christian pilgrims from neighboring Mexican villages who had come for their daily worship and a handful of tourists like me who had come to visit the basilica for the first time.

The basilica complex is located on a massive rectangular stone plaza at the foot of Tepeyac Hill, surrounded by a low wall with built-in seats for weary travelers. On the far side stood the New Basilica, a modern oval tent-shaped

---

[4] Carroll, "Honoring Christopher Columbus".

[5] Fray Diego Durán, *The History of the Indies of New Spain*, trans. Doris Heyden (Norman and London: University of Oklahoma Press, 1994), 190.

[6] David Roos, "Human Sacrifice: Why the Aztecs Practiced This Gory Ritual", History, October 11, 2018, https://www.history.com/news/aztec-human-sacrifice-religion.

building adorned with a massive cross and open on nearly all sides so visitors could enter from almost anywhere. Adjacent to the New Basilica stood the Old Basilica with its dingy red brick and dusty golden domes, but it was closed to the public at that time while repairs were being made to its sinking foundation. The palm trees surrounding the plaza shone in bright green hues, and bronze statues glimmered in the sun.

As I took in the scene around me, my attention focused on an elderly woman kneeling on the plaza. Her head was bowed. She clutched a rosary as she shuffled slowly across the stone plaza on her knees toward the New Basilica, the sun beating down on her. Her journey must have been several hundred painful yards. A slow, kneeling shuffle across the plaza to the New Basilica is a tradition among Catholic pilgrims and locals in Mexico, an approach that shows a posture of humility before God and gratitude for Mary's intercession in prayer on their behalf. I was struck by the woman's dedication to the faith. I knelt to experience this act of devotion for myself, shuffling my knees slowly as I'd seen her do. After about five feet, I knew it was not for me—or my knees.

Paul, Gabe, Father Mike, and I entered the basilica from the front and gently pushed our way through the crowd toward the altar. As my eyes adjusted to the dimly lit cathedral, I noticed women kneeling in reverence, men standing with their heads bowed, and, above the altar, a vibrant image of the Blessed Virgin Mary. Even from as far away as the back of the church, I was struck by how clearly I could see the 400-year-old imprint, as if I were staring at a real woman, not the likeness of one. Father Mike took us behind the altar to a lower level, where we stepped onto a moving walkway that passed in front of Juan Diego's tilma from below. The walkway allowed the frequent Masses to continue undisturbed and prevented tourists from lingering too long. I stared at the image of Mary as we approached slowly from the side and noted how the details were just as clear from odd angles as they were from directly in front, though the color seemed to change slightly as we passed before her.

The image depicts Mary standing humbly, her hands in prayer, eyes downcast. Rays of light burst all around her, and she stands on a crescent moon held up by a cherub. Father Mike later explained the symbolism in both Aztec paganism and the Bible. Sun rays are a nod to the Aztec sun god, Huitzilopochtli, known as the greatest and most powerful god in Aztec culture. Mary stands in front of the sunburst with a black cross at her neck, showing that the one true God she proclaims eclipses the power of the Aztec sun god. The moon is associated with the Tezcatlipoca, the Aztec god who represents darkness and night. Mary's position on top of the moon represents her God's triumph over darkness and evil.

Father Mike explained that Catholics interpret the woman in Revelation who was "clothed with the sun, with the moon under her feet" (Rev 12:1) as Mary, the Mother of Christ. He said, "Isn't it interesting how perfectly the symbolism of the image would have spoken to the pagan Aztec culture at that time while communicating the truth of the one true God?"

I rode that belt probably ten times, unable to absorb what I was seeing before my eyes: an ancient relic, somehow youthful in its luster, yet nearly 400 years old, with colors so crisp that they challenged every preconceived notion I'd carried with me that morning. How could a poor native's tilma made of hemp fibers—one that would have usually deteriorated completely in 30 years—still be here hundreds of years later? And with such a meaningful and radiant image? I was trying to retain my historical perspective, still holding faith at arm's length.

I wasn't praying much anymore in those days, but as I stood still and silent before the tilma, I slipped into a state of wonderment and awe before God—a kind of meditation that felt a lot like prayer to me at the time. I chose to believe, if only for a moment, that I really was standing face to face with a miracle hanging on a wall, just feet in front of me. Words from the Gospel that I had heard as a boy came to mind: "Behold your mother." Seeing his mother, Mary, from the cross, Jesus uttered these precious words to the Beloved Disciple (John). I first learned about the scene when my parents explained how they had entrusted my brothers and me to the care of Our Lady at our baptisms. How long ago that seemed.

The moving sidewalk and the area surrounding the altar were crammed with people quietly observing the image on the tilma. I stepped off the sidewalk for the last time and headed for an empty pew off to the right of the altar as far back as I could go, away from the crowds. I sat down, still puzzled by what I had seen, and for the first time in a long time, I found myself truly alone. Tunnel vision blocked the hustle and bustle all around me. I no longer heard the whispers. Where 500 people gathered in curiosity and worship, I sat alone with the image of the woman I'd known about my whole life but couldn't understand. The silence brought an unwelcome emptiness, and it made me uncomfortable.

I buried my head in my hands. Then something happened that I can hardly explain. Inwardly I heard clear and strong: "Why are you hurting me?"

What the hell was that? I listened closely, waiting for my cue, as I did in the hospitals when code calls came over the PA system. My heart raced with adrenaline as I waited to hear my next instruction. *Do I need to respond? Is this an emergency? Does someone need my help?*

But nothing came. The medical student in me calmed down as I came back to the present. Shaking myself away from the hospital scene in my mind, I became uncomfortable as I remembered I was sitting in a place of worship. I nervously scanned the faces in the pews around me, searching for the owner of the voice or any indication that someone else had heard the booming question as well. The young woman in front of me knelt silently, head bowed, her lips moving slightly as she clasped her rosary. A man several rows behind me sat in a prayerful, undisturbed posture. Two elderly women slowly approached the pew behind me, making the sign of the cross as they genuflected by the pew. These were certainly not the faces of people who had heard this striking question, let alone posed it in the first place.

I pondered the question "Why are you hurting me? *What does that even mean? I'm studying to be a doctor. I don't hurt people. I heal people.*

I dismissed whatever voice I thought I'd heard. It must have been the heat, or the *cerveza* I'd had at lunch. Either way, my faith life was lousy, and I knew it. I couldn't possibly have heard a voice from God.

Paul, Gabe, and Father Mike found me in the pew and suggested we move to the balcony that hung over packed pews in the main seating area. Father Mike offered to say a special Mass just for us. It had been several months since I'd participated in Mass. I'd figured I'd sit through a few Masses during my time in Mexico, but my long absence from the Church was bothering me more than I had thought it would.

When it came time to receive the Eucharist, Father Mike placed the Host on my tongue. My stomach began to turn. Sweat beads formed across my forehead and my hands felt clammy. I knew I was doing something hypocritical. I was not living my faith, especially if this was Jesus' Body and Blood.

Then, the scientist in me kicked in again, and I dismissed the physical illness in my gut. I probably just needed fresh air. After Mass, Father, Mike, Gabe, Paul, and I left the balcony area and headed for the nearest exit. I couldn't wait for the warm breeze to break the stale air inside the Basilica. But before we stepped out of the church, I turned for one last view of the tilma as the voice rang again in my mind.

Late that night, I awoke to a frantic knock on the front door. I heard footsteps heading to answer, but I stepped into the hallway anyway to see if I could help. A young man with bloodshot eyes stood outside the door, reeking of alcohol. Father Pedro, one of the other young priests at Father Mike's rectory, told me the young man's mother was dying. He was so overcome with the grief of losing her that he had self-medicated with alcohol to quell his pain, but he came to his senses just in time to ask that a priest visit the hospital to offer her Last Rites, pray for her, and comfort her. I asked Father Pedro if I could accompany him, thinking it might be safer for him to travel in a pair.

In my short time there, I'd learned that Mexico City was not the safest place for Catholic priests. Though many people in Mexico were Catholic, the secular Mexican government had a long history of oppressing the Catholic Church. During periods of fierce anticlericalism, priests had been arrested, tortured, and executed without trial. Although priests were currently being tolerated, corrupt transit cops were known to target them in traffic, extorting money for permission to access certain roads. Some priests, Father Pedro told me, feared being abducted and imprisoned by authorities under false accusations. Having grown up in a place where no one walked alone at night, I was ready to accompany Father Pedro through any late-night danger on the streets. In addition, as a medical student, I couldn't help but wonder how the local city hospital cared for people at the end of life. My fascination with medicine called me, even at such an early hour in the morning.

We arrived safely at a dark and dilapidated city hospital. Lights flickered inside the massive concrete building. Many hallway entrances were veiled with plastic tarps, still awaiting reconstruction after the earthquake that had shaken the city two years earlier. Crumbled cement crunched under my feet as we climbed several flights of stairs to the intensive care unit. Peering through patient-room windows as I followed Father Pedro down the hallway, I noticed glass bottles dripping saline solution in place of IV bags—an outdated practice.

The ICU was a multiple-occupancy room with a dozen beds. I glanced through the glass window to see a frail woman propped up in one of the beds, lying still with her eyes closed, covered by a wool blanket. A handful of puffy-eyed loved ones encircled her, including the young man who'd knocked on the rectory door earlier. Before entering the room, Father Pedro removed his stole from his pocket. He kissed the embroidered image of the cross and hung the purple cloth around his neck and shoulders, where it draped past his waist.

While he administered the sacraments and visited with the family, I paced the hospital hallways, struck by the poor condition of the medical facility and equipment. My ears were accustomed to the rhythmic beeps of monitors in hospitals, the sounds of life. In this hospital, there were no beeping heart monitors, just distant moans and otherwise, silence.

I strolled to the edge of the hallway, where a giant tarp hung in place of a wall, a meager separation between the sick patients in the hospital and the densely polluted Mexico City air. I stood in front of the plastic veil, a dusty breeze passing freely through the tattered tarp and touching my face. I peered between the hallway's end and the sheet, down several flights of darkness and neglected buildings, still in shambles with little hope of repair after the earthquake of 1985. One too many steps and I would have been in for a long fall. Frayed wires twisted from the walls' edges, and rubble lay scattered across the ground level in an eerie stillness—a sight that sent a shiver down my spine and shook me from my sleepy stupor.

I slipped into thought as I made my way back to the ICU, remembering the stillness I had felt earlier that day before the image of Our Lady of Guadalupe. And then, the mysterious voice: "Why are you hurting me?"

I reviewed my certainty of the strange event in my head. Yes, I was sure the voice was audible, and I was nearly positive the voice was speaking to me. But who was speaking to me? *Was it Jesus? Was it Mary? Was it my subconscious? What did this voice mean? Whom am I hurting?*

As quickly as these questions began racing through my head again, I stamped them out. It was easier to ignore the voice and my imagination. How else could a physician-in-training explain something so unusual?

I stood by the ICU window as Father Pedro wrapped up his visit. With his eyes closed and his hands on the sick woman's shoulder, he prayed for her. There was something simple about this moment, and yet something mysterious, too.

I realized that both the doctor and the priest are ministers of healing. A doctor cares for the body, and a priest cares for the soul. The doctor tends to physical pain and

suffering, and the priest tends to spiritual pain and suffering. The doctor is concerned primarily with the quality of
our earthly existence, while the priest is concerned ultimately with *where* we will exist for all eternity.

I was a healthy young man at the cusp of career success.
I certainly wasn't lying on my deathbed. But somehow I
related to this woman and her need for Father Pedro. A
longing arose in my heart for what she was receiving: care
for her soul.

In the ruins of the broken building, and beholding the
ruin of this woman's earthly body, I felt a peace I hadn't
felt in more years than I could remember, and yet, still, I
failed to comprehend its source.

6

Following Procedure

1987–Norfolk, Virginia

Abigail, one of the patients in our OB clinic at Norfolk General Hospital, asked me at a routine prenatal appointment if her belly looked too big. She had never been pregnant before, and she had become concerned after one of her in-laws had recently blurted out how huge her belly was. She asked me to measure her again to make sure nothing was wrong.

She leaned back slowly on the exam chair and I stretched a soft tape measure across her abdomen. She was 29 weeks along and measured several centimeters ahead of schedule, so I ordered an ultrasound.

The images confirmed a tragic abnormality. The fetus' head was growing at a rate faster than normal, with a skull circumference measuring closer to that of a 35-week fetus—the size of a grapefruit rather than the normal baseball size for this gestational age.

It appeared to be a severe case of hydrocephalus, a condition in which cerebrospinal fluid accumulates in the brain and can cause minor to severe brain damage. Abigail came to our OB/GYN clinic because she did not have medical insurance, and our clinic took uninsured patients in the Tidewater area who would not be seen by other private practices. Because she came late to care, as many patients without a primary health plan often did, I had no way of knowing how long the excess fluid had been present.

I walked over to the resident's central office and called in Dr. Rose for his opinion and to discuss a treatment plan.

During my residency, I worked under the direction of several attending physicians, but Dr. Rose was one of my favorites. He was an excellent professor and always available to share knowledge, answer questions, and work side by side with residents if needed. But he was more than a medical mentor. He taught me how to care for the entire person by considering not only a woman's biological and medical factors, but also the unique psychological and social factors of her particular situation. I noticed that he treated each patient with compassion and offered the same time and attention to uninsured patients as he did to paying patients. And they seemed to love him for his good bedside manner and subtle sense of humor.

Dr. Rose was a maternal-fetal medicine specialist, which meant after his traditional obstetrics and gynecology education, he had received additional training to learn how to treat medical complications related to pregnancy. He was the go-to doctor for patients with high-risk pregnancies who came to the clinic. Under his guidance, I learned to treat patients experiencing preterm labor, gestational diabetes, hypertension, and lifestyle risk factors such as obesity, drug use, and smoking. And then there were the chromosomal abnormalities he treated: Down syndrome and other trisomy disorders or birth defects, including spina bifida, anencephaly, hydrocephalus, and cystic hygroma. He saw the most extreme cases, which other doctors in the region could not or would not take, patients from Norfolk to Richmond and down to North Carolina across Chapel Hill, Kitty Hawk, and the Outer Banks. I was thankful to learn so much about how to care for patients with high-risk pregnancies under his mentorship.

Dr. Rose examined the ultrasound photos closely and confirmed my diagnosis. The black oval shape in the center represented the fluid collecting inside the skull. Squished between the fluid and the skull bone was only about a 1-millimeter [0.04-inch] rim of gray matter, representing the damaged brain. He measured the gray matter against the skull. The less gray matter there was, the worse the hydrocephalus.

"There's a lot of fluid," Dr. Rose said. "See how the brain is being pushed to the periphery here?" He pointed to the gray matter.

"Yes, I see that," I responded.

"We don't know how much brain function has already been damaged, but it's likely significant."

"What would you say for treatment?" I asked, assuming he'd recommend shunting, the placement of a small, flexible tube and valve system in the brain to drain excess fluid into the stomach where it can be absorbed back into the bloodstream. Mild to moderate cases of hydrocephalus can be treated after birth in this way.

"We have had good results with shunting to relieve the pressure so the tissue can return to its normal position," he answered, and paused before continuing. "However, this appears to be beyond the scope of hope for any normal cognitive outcome for this fetus."

Though most babies born with severe hydrocephalus who receive medical treatment survive and go on to live normal lives, Dr. Rose thought the chances of thriving outside the womb for this baby were slim, because we saw almost no remaining brain tissue. Most babies with scans like this die shortly after birth or live in an unresponsive state. The child would likely have significant long-term brain damage.

"Does that mean we will recommend termination?" I asked Dr. Rose.

"Yes. Give her all the options, but explain the benefits of a D&X in her situation. It's probably the best thing she can do for herself and her child."

"D&X" is a colloquial term for a dilation and extraction, a type of termination procedure that would later become commonly known as a "partial-birth abortion" and banned with the 2003 Partial-Birth Abortion Ban Act.

I returned to the exam room where Abigail was waiting in dread for the life-shattering news I was about to deliver. "Abigail, I'm sorry to say that the ultrasound images detected an abnormality in your child's brain." I pulled up the images on the screen and pointed to the fluid in the center, explaining that the brain tissue was being destroyed, and if the fluid continued to collect inside the skull at a rapid rate, it could be risky for her to carry to term.

She stared at the wall over my shoulder, unable to speak. Tears welled up in her eyes.

"I know this was unexpected. I'm so sorry, Abigail." I offered her a fistful of tissues and let her cry as long as she needed to. Then she looked to me for guidance. "What should I do for my baby girl?" she asked.

I knew it was my responsibility to answer the question both morally and medically—her question was both moral and medical. I explained she could carry to term and let the child live or die naturally, but that most children with this condition die shortly after birth in a great deal of pain, and she'd have to undergo a C-section because of the size of the child's head. If the child did survive, she would require shunting, which could possibly restore brain function. But this would be a very expensive option and a burden for someone with minimal means. Even with the surgery, it was likely the child would have

a profound cognitive deficit and a life of pain and suffering. Or she could opt for a dilation and extraction, which
carried the risk of hemorrhage and of damage to her cervix and uterus. It was a tremendously difficult option to
offer a mother, but at least she would never have to see
her baby suffer.

I watched as countless emotions cycled across Abigail's face: love for her unborn daughter, concern for her
daughter's well-being, fear of the unknown, dread of the
heartache she was already beginning to feel and that would
certainly continue. This was a mother overwhelmed with
horrible news with no one else to turn to but us. And we
didn't have enough hope to offer her—just a long list of
horrific unknowns.

After several minutes of discussing the pros and cons of
each option, she agreed that termination carried the lowest
risk and, in her view, was the least cruel option. It broke
my heart every time a mother made this gut-wrenching
decision. I tried to comfort her by assuring her she was
doing the best thing for her daughter, but even I wasn't so
sure anymore.

The following week at the hospital, Dr. Rose and I prepared for Abigail's procedure. Before any abortion, I felt
like a soldier suiting up for battle. I had to get in the zone,
setting my own opinions and feelings to the side, replaying
my training until I felt confident and ready to complete
the task before me.

Abigail had been at the hospital overnight while her
cervix was dilated with laminaria, a type of seaweed ster-
ilized and dried into a small stick. As the seaweed absorbs
moisture, it expands and slowly opens the cervix. When
she reached about 4 centimeters, the nurses began Pitocin
to jumpstart her contractions.

When Abigail was sufficiently dilated, Dr. Rose and
I entered the operating room. One nurse arranged our

surgical instruments on the tray next to us while another checked her IV.

"Good morning, Abigail, how are you feeling?" I asked.

"I'm OK. A little tired," she said, sighing. She wasn't in much pain since she had received an epidural, but I noticed her eyes were red and puffy. Perhaps it was from poor sleep the night before. Or crying. Or both. I could only imagine her despair.

"I understand. This will be quick, and you shouldn't feel too much. Just a little pressure," I assured her as I gently pressed on her stomach to check the position of the baby.

After easing her lower legs into the stirrups, I sat down on my stool and rolled forward. Next I prepped her skin with antiseptic. I reminded myself to stay focused on the procedure and not to think too much about the reality of what we were about to do. *Whatever quick pain the child will feel in the next few moments would pale in comparison to a lifetime of suffering*, I told myself.

The ultrasound machine next to her bed provided second-by-second images for Dr. Rose and me to refer to as we worked so we could see where the head and all the parts were in relation to each other and the placenta. Dr. Rose supervised close behind and directed me to reach into her cervix.

With the help of the ultrasound machine, I identified a fetal leg and pulled it steadily through the cervical opening with the amniotic membrane intact. While I kept the fetal limb in place, a nurse assistant handed me an amniotic hook. I rolled my stool slightly to the side and peered around the blue drapes, which prevented Abigail from seeing what we were doing. "I'm going to break your water now. You're going to feel a big gush."

I poked the membrane enough to rupture it. As amniotic fluid poured into a plastic bag at the edge of the gurney in front of me, I pulled the fetal legs down and out of the cervix as far as I could. Nearly the entire child was exposed up to the shoulders, with her back facing the ceiling. Dr. Rose directed me to keep the baby face down and nestle her skull up against the cervix.

Dr. Rose moved in front of me and asked me to follow his lead. Our hands worked together. I helped him by holding the fetus' legs in place, constantly feeling calves and feet, thighs and knees, fighting my grip. Dr. Rose held a pair of surgical scissors, checking the monitor as he carefully inserted them into the cervix. I held my breath for what was to happen next.

Dr. Rose gave a firm jab to drain fluid from the base of the fetal skull.

"How are you doing, Abigail?" I asked, probably to distract myself as much as her.

She nodded sluggishly.

"You're doing great. We're almost done."

I held the fluttering legs tightly as Dr. Rose continued to work. He placed the suction through the hole he had made in the base of the scull to vacuum out brain tissue. Then the tiny legs went limp. With enough fluid and tissue removed to complete the delivery, we pulled the fetus through the cervix with forceps. Dr. Rose quickly transferred the body to a large bucket on the operating table. We turned our attention to delivering the placenta. Dr. Rose asked me to check the cervix for any lacerations that might have been caused by pulling the fetus feet first. The cervix was intact without tears, and bleeding was normal.

"We're all done, Abigail," I said as I pulled off my gloves and rolled my chair back. My announcement was met with silence. I stood up and saw that her eyes were closed and her cheeks were soaked with tears.

My first year of residency included several months of internal medicine and emergency room work. Over the full four years, I spent blocks of time each year in obstetrics, delivering babies and caring for pregnant women, and gynecology, which involved caring for patients with conditions such as pelvic infections, abnormal bleeding, and ovarian cysts. Gynecology also included surgery, "open" cases through incisions—to gain visualization and accommodate the surgeon's hands—and "closed" cases called laparoscopies, which are performed through tiny incisions with long slender instruments, using a small camera for visualization on a large computer monitor.

I wanted to be a well-rounded doctor and learn everything I could about all facets of OB/GYN and reproductive health. In the past, this specialty focused on caring for pregnant women and their unborn babies and on women's gynecologic problems. But as technology advanced and the sexual revolution of the 1960s led to wider acceptance of contraception and abortion, the OB/GYN standard of care expanded to include all sorts of reproductive health care services, including birth control, sterilization, infertility treatment, hormone therapy, and abortion. Even though abortion was not practiced by a majority of OB/GYNs at the time, I was open to all these aspects of my field and wanted to be competent in every area.

I treated menstrual cycle irregularities and menopause. I made incisions and performed laparoscopies. I treated endometriosis and cervical cancer and ectopic pregnancies. I cared for in vitro fertilization patients and delivered babies vaginally and by C-sections. I placed IUDs and tied tubes. I prescribed contraception and terminated pregnancies.

We residents performed abortions alongside attending OB/GYNs and by ourselves for all kinds of reasons, but we were not there to offer elective abortions for convenience. Women went to abortion clinics for that. At Eastern Virginia Medical School, we believed abortions should be safe and rare. We were permitted to perform abortions only in the case of life-threatening fetal diseases or when the life of the mother was in jeopardy. But as it sometimes happens in practice, the definition of "life-threatening" was expanded to include fetal deformities such as spina bifida and hydrocephalus—conditions whose severity varies widely. Some cases were treatable and potentially not life-threatening. Rather than trying to treat the disease, we often opted to terminate the pregnancy on the general rationale of preventing pain and suffering.

We performed these abortions usually by dilation and curettage (D&C) in the first trimester, by sweeping out the contents of the uterus with a noose-shaped curette. Dilation and evacuations (D&Es), which involve a vacuum suction and forceps to break apart the fetal tissue before it is removed from the uterus, were common in the early second trimester, usually between 14 and 18 weeks. Usually after 18 weeks, when the fetus was more mature and difficult to break apart, we injected prostaglandin chemicals or saline into the mother's abdomen and poisoned the fetus with salt to induce labor. Saline is no longer used today because it can be dangerous to the mother. We now have more effective medication to stimulate labor without saline. We were also just beginning to use potassium chloride to stop the fetal heart before delivery in these cases, but that was rare.

Children with life-limiting diseases were usually aborted by inducing a premature delivery in the second trimester and allowing them to die "naturally", since their lungs were underdeveloped and unable to get enough oxygen. In these cases, the baby was often put in a bucket on the floor by the edge of the gurney, covered with a surgical towel, and immediately whisked out of the room. Dilation and extraction (D&X) when the fetus is aborted in the process of being delivered, was beginning to be used in the late second trimester and early third trimester, particularly for babies with hydrocephalus like Abigail's.

Dr. Rose showed me how to terminate safely and carefully for the mother's health. He kept his hands on mine during the procedures, guiding me, just like Dr. Cohen had in medical school. "Adjust forceps this way," he'd say. "Turn the curette this way."

I felt for the parents of these sick babies. Many of them had exhausted every avenue of medical help and done everything in their power to avoid an abortion, but in the end, they felt like they didn't have a choice.

But I also worried whether or not their choices would haunt them for the rest of their lives. Would they ever find peace? Some patients asked for the ashes or their baby's handprints and footprints. Others invited priests to baptize the babies who survived for a few moments outside the womb. Some just wanted to forget. They each had their own way of coping, and I trusted they would all eventually find healing for their broken hearts by believing they did the right thing.

I wanted to help women, and I wanted to be the doctor women came to for help. I thought that meant I had to know how to do abortions and how to do them well. Yet I was still sensitive to the reality of what we were doing to unborn children. My heart always sank when I saw a fetus lurch away from my surgical instruments on the ultrasound machine or when squirming limbs in my grasp went limp. It was never easy for me to terminate, because I knew deep down in my heart that a human life was on the other end of my instruments.

For the sick babies with a life-limiting diagnosis, sometimes I couldn't help but wonder if abortion was really the best treatment we had to offer. How could ending a life be considered "treatment" when we were taught as doctors to do no harm? And would ending the life of her child, no matter how sick, be something a mother could ever get over emotionally? I asked Dr. Rose this question, and he pointed to the literature that said women do not experience any lasting emotional problems after an abortion. Women have a right to choose abortion, he said, and doctors need to know how to perform abortions safely.

Dr. Rose traced his finger over the ultrasound screen in his office. "See this here?" he asked me, pointing to a small white line and a blot on the screen. "This is the spine, and you can see the opening right here."

My patient's 20-week-old fetus was showing signs of spina bifida, an opening of the spinal cord that can cause paralysis of the lower limbs and, in some cases, severe cognitive impairment.

For a few months during my residency, Dr. Rose and I studied ultrasound videos of unborn children with spinal abnormalities, examining the difference between the lower and upper limb movements. Often, the arms would move much like those of a normal fetus, but the legs would twitch randomly, or they might not move at all.

I always hoped to see normal movement in the lower extremities. Legs with some movement usually meant the baby would be carried to term and treated. Legs with no movement usually meant the pregnancy was destined for termination. The termination of a wanted pregnancy is a terrible choice no parent wants to make, so I would wait with laser-focused anticipation for those legs to move.

Dr. Rose's goal in the spina bifida study was to learn more about which pregnancies he could help and save. The study would help predict which cases had a higher chance of correction or reduced risk of complications with surgery after birth and which cases would lead to poor quality of life and suffering even with surgery. Though abortion was always an option he hoped to avoid, Dr. Rose believed that abortion was a necessary procedure in the world of obstetrics and that high-risk doctors had no choice but to become proficient in the unfortunate methods of pregnancy termination. Every profession had its downside, he supposed, and this was ours.

Nevertheless, Dr. Rose treated every case with care and informed his patients of their options and the advantages and disadvantages of each. In the most severe cases, his patients often chose abortion due to the suffering and low quality of life the children were expected to have. Naturally, parents-to-be struggled in imagining their child in pain and confined to a wheelchair, unable to run with the other kids at school or speak or learn normally and requiring assistance for basic functions like dressing and using the bathroom. Today, we celebrate when courageous individuals defy the odds and overcome immense challenges with unending fortitude, but I wasn't focused on the possibilities of these children at the time. Bereaved mothers and fathers could not see through the pain and uncertainty of their present circumstances to a hopeful future.

Sadly, many patients in the spina bifida study tearfully chose abortion after seeing the lack of lower limb function on the ultrasounds, and Dr. Rose and I always supported their decisions.

I hoped the patient whose ultrasound images we were studying would have a chance to save her child through surgery after birth, but from the looks of the ultrasound, I could tell this case was more severe. Dr. Rose explained that the opening on the fetal spine and lack of leg movement indicated the child would likely experience a very low quality of life. Although you can't always know exactly how severely affected the fetus will be until some time after birth, Dr. Rose thought this child would likely suffer for the duration of life, and he emphasized our inability to make a long-term prognosis. There were many unknowns, but suffering for the child was almost certain.

I delivered the heartbreaking news to my patient at her appointment the next day. There were tears and tissues and a heartbreaking conversation about her options: carry to term and treat with surgery, with the risk of a lifetime of medical complications and suffering, or a termination of the pregnancy by early delivery. She rambled, through her tears, about this baby they very much wanted but didn't want to suffer. Ultimately, she put her full trust in my recommendation for an early delivery as her best option to spare her baby, herself, and her family needless suffering.

When Dr. Rose sensed I was feeling uneasy about aborting a fetus who had been diagnosed with a life-threatening illness, he would show me the damage done by the defect or disease—on the ultrasound or by examining the delivered baby—to help me feel better about the abortion. Some days, his assurance worked. I reasoned that we really were helping a child avoid a life of suffering, and maybe abortions could be a good thing under certain circumstances. Other days, I felt more tempted to mourn the innocent lives lost at our clinic. But then I would reason that the job would be done by Dr. Rose or another resident whether I was present or not. *Did it matter who held the curette or administered the abortion drug? The outcome would be the same*, I told myself.

I'd always settled my conscience by assuring myself: *We are following protocol. We are eliminating suffering and practicing excellent medicine. This is merciful. This is what I have to learn to do to be a good doctor.* I desperately wanted to be proud of my work, and that led me to make concessions I'd never thought I would make.

Over time, my heart became like steel, hard and unyielding. The voice I had heard at the Basilica of Our Lady of Guadalupe in Mexico City—"Why are you hurting me?"—was just a memory. I pressed on with more abortions, linked arm in arm with the medical status quo.

7

Double Life

1988

One warm spring morning, after a stressful overnight shift in residency at Norfolk General Hospital, I put my Honda station wagon in gear and headed straight for the open road toward Virginia Beach. Driving took the edge off and helped me decompress when my mind was whirling from the fast-paced decision-making of hospital life. The waves and salty air quieted my mind. I began the 15-mile drive east to the ocean while making my best effort to turn off the never-ending stream of patient-related thoughts in my head.

A sign listing the businesses in a shopping center caught my eye while I was stopped at a light. Witchduck Road Pregnancy Center was one of them. My effort to keep the work side of my brain turned off was quickly derailed. I was curious to learn about the pregnancy center, so I took a sharp left turn, parked, and went inside.

The space was homey and welcoming, with warm colors on the walls and soft couches in the waiting area. A young woman stood up from her desk and walked toward me, greeting me with a gentle smile. "Welcome to Witchduck Road Pregnancy Center. What brings you in today?"

I told her I was a resident doctor in OB/GYN at Eastern Virginia School of Medicine and that I wanted to know more about what goes on in a pregnancy center. Her eyes lit up.

"It's not every day we have a doctor drop in!" She explained that many of their patients are in crisis pregnancy situations. The staff of the pregnancy center would inform them of their choices and help them navigate challenges such as absent partners or financial difficulties. "Let me show you around."

She eagerly led me into the business area where two volunteers sat filing paperwork. Down a hallway were several comfortable counseling rooms. I noticed there were no desks in these rooms, just a simple chair and a couch in each and screens to show educational videos about pregnancy. A larger room was filled with neatly organized baby gear and supplies: bassinets and strollers on one side, bins of toys on the other, and neat stacks of clothes and diapers organized by size on the shelves. In the hallway was a resource wall with rows of brochures on all sorts of topics: fetal development, complications of abortion, and chastity. The atmosphere was gentle and inviting, opposite to the sterility and stress in the hospital environment to which I had become accustomed.

I was impressed with their space and the free resources they offered women in our community. But it was the warmth and gentleness of the volunteers—and the fact they were *volunteers*—that tipped me off that this was a special place. I asked her why they do the work they do.

"Well, we believe the Word of God calls us to do this—to love the women in our community by meeting these needs."

I smiled and nodded my head. It had been a while since I had heard someone speak so openly and naturally about God like that. I was reminded of my parents speaking about God this way when I was young.

She didn't tell me it was a pro-life center, but the bro-chure topics were pro-life, and I connected the dots during our conversation. Though I didn't consider myself pro-life, at least not in every circumstance, I identified with these volunteers and their work because of my parents' emphasis on the sanctity of life. Without giving it much thought, I offered to volunteer. "Is there anything I can do to help?" I asked.

"Yes! Our director would be thrilled to have you come in one evening to meet her. I'm sure she'll have lots of ideas about how you can help."

We set up a time for me to meet the director and said our goodbyes.

"The Holy Spirit works in funny ways," she said, laugh-ing, as I waved and walked out the door.

She was kind, nonjudgmental, and put my heart at ease. I didn't see much conflict between my residency work and volunteering in the pregnancy center. I had always had a heart for serving the underserved in my community. I was helping women at the hospital, and I would be helping women at the pregnancy center—just in different ways. I didn't expect that I would soon find my two worlds in such powerful opposition to each other and that the ten-sion would slowly tear my heart in two.

A few weeks had passed since my initial meeting at the pregnancy center when I was suddenly derailed by one of the most devastating abortions of my residency. It still makes my stomach churn to think about it. The case was an unfortunate reminder of the fear that drove so many women to end their pregnancies.

Several weeks earlier, a woman named Katie had received the results of her genetic screening. The bloodwork indi-cated a possible chromosomal abnormality based on her hormone levels. She had low levels of alpha-fetoprotein and estriol and higher levels of human chorionic gonadotropin (hCG). While this triple screen doesn't test for specific genetic abnormalities, I explained that her results indicated an increased risk for Down syndrome, or possibly trisomy 18 or 13.

I told her and her boyfriend, Jason, that while it can be concerning to receive these results, they shouldn't worry yet, since the results of the screen themselves aren't necessarily indicative of a birth defect. We would be able to get a better idea of her baby's health with more tests at her 20-week ultrasound appointment.

Katie, who was usually chatty, appeared shell-shocked and unable to speak. She said she didn't have any questions and seemed eager to wrap up the appointment. I left feeling uneasy about her shift in energy, but I knew I had done my best to explain to her and her partner that she needed further testing to confirm her baby's condition.

A few weeks later, Katie and Jason came back to the clinic. She was there to tell me she had decided to terminate her pregnancy, because she couldn't handle the chance of having a child with a diagnosis like Down syndrome. I reiterated to her that the information in the blood test was limited. It only indicated an increased risk of Down, not a certainty. Considering the mother's young age, the chances of delivering a baby with Down syndrome were only 1 in 1,200. It was more likely her baby was totally healthy. If she waited just a few weeks longer, we could perform amniocentesis, a diagnostic test done by inserting a needle into her abdomen and drawing a sample of amniotic fluid to confirm or deny Down.

Her eyes darted around the room as I spoke to her. Her heels swung back and forth, tapping the bottom of the exam chair quietly.

"While your baby is in the statistical group for the *possibility* of having a chromosomal condition, your triple screen test results alone do not prove there is anything wrong with your pregnancy."

"The risk is just too much for me," she said.

Her boyfriend turned to her. "Are you sure you want to go through with this, Katie? I told you how I feel about it."

"Yes, I'm sure. I just can't handle the possibility."

"It's your decision, not mine," he said, folding his arms.

This was the first time I had witnessed the father and the mother disagreeing about the decision to abort. I felt for Jason and was uneasy about Katie's decision. It wasn't often that a patient made a decision before we could run an amniocentesis or do an anatomy scan.

I wondered if there were other factors playing into her decision that I didn't know about. Maybe she was already on the fence about keeping the pregnancy, and the test results had just pushed her over the edge. Maybe she had realized she didn't feel ready to be a mother after all, and the genetic risk brought out unexpected fear in her: fear of her child suffering, fear of being overwhelmed, fear of the unknown. Anything could have led to her decision, and it was not my job to pry. I stuck to the medical facts and said all I felt comfortable saying to discourage a decision this early in her pregnancy. But ultimately, her boyfriend was right: it was up to her.

In the delivery room a few days later, Katie's contractions were getting closer together. Her boyfriend reached for her hand and gave it a tight squeeze. After laboring through the morning, she was ready to push.

After Katie delivered, I examined her baby's body up and down, looking for indicators of Down or another chromosomal abnormality: a small or unusually shaped head, the distinctive eye slants, a single crease across the palm. For a moment, I had almost hoped to find them. At least, for Katie, any hint of a defect might ease the weight of her decision and help her move on with her life.

If we saw the signs of Down syndrome in situations like this, we would let the patient know. But it would not have been customary to explain that the anatomy associated with Down was *not* detected unless the patient asked. And Katie did not ask. She did not ask to hold or see her child.

In a sense, I thought it was a gift for her not to know. She would grieve the loss of her pregnancy, but eventually she would go on to live believing she had spared her baby a life of difficulty and pain. She would live believing that she had done what was best for her baby.

But the same was not true for me. I did not have the benefit of ignorance. As I searched for signs of chromosomal abnormality in the face and body of this tiny being, I found instead 10 perfectly formed fingers and toes and a perfectly shaped head and eyes and nose and ears: the perfect proportions of a developing body. And I knew that that day I had ended the life of a completely healthy 18-week fetus with no genetic abnormalities.

I placed the baby in the warmer next to the gurney where it quickly died. Jason, the father, stood over his child with a blank stare.

This moment was too much for my heart to handle. Perhaps I would have felt crushed if the baby *did* have Down syndrome as well, but knowing that my patient had made a life-ending decision based on insufficient medical information was a reality I could no longer ignore.

As a doctor, I wanted to be better for my patients—the mothers, the babies, *and* the fathers. But I felt powerless. The decisions were not up to me; they were up to the mothers. Questions swirled inside my mind. What was my responsibility to the baby in this situation? And what was my responsibility to the father of this little life, especially as the best interests of them all seemed to conflict with one another? Must I provide a procedure when I don't agree that the situation justifies the ending of an innocent human life?

I shuddered to think that fear and the desire for "perfect" and healthy babies were driving many of the mothers' decisions that I had signed off on. Regardless, I continued to push my conscience aside and go along with the difficult realities of my work as an OB/GYN.

Before I knew it, it was time to head back to the pregnancy center to meet the executive director. During the drive, I thought of Katie and the events surrounding her decision. Jason holding Katie's hand. The baby in my hand who was rejected for fear of imperfection. Would Katie later regret her decision? Would Jason resent her for it?

The tormenting thoughts fled my mind as soon as I walked in the door of the pregnancy center. The office was abuzz with conversation and soft background music. The executive director greeted me with a bright, dimpled smile. "Hi, I'm Maggie Sharpe."

We shook hands and I introduced myself.

"We're thrilled to have you here tonight, Dr. Bruchalski. Our first client is scheduled to come in soon," she said and turned to a group of volunteers gathered behind her. "I hope you don't mind, but our staff usually opens in prayer before our evening appointments."

"Not at all," I said.

She reached for my hand, and I joined her and four other female volunteers in the prayer circle. They took turns praying for their clients and what they called their "divine appointments". One volunteer asked that the women would be made more aware of the life inside them. One prayed that her clients would view what they might think is a curse as a blessing, so the babies could be born and loved. Another asked that the Holy Spirit would bring those God wanted into the center that day and that they would be up for the challenge of caring for their crisis pregnancies. Maggie spontaneously chimed in with "Yes, God" and "Praise you, Jesus."

Praying in a free-form style like this wasn't something I was used to, but I enjoyed hearing how much they cared for the women who would soon step into their office. They had faith God could change the hearts of their clients who were considering abortion. For a doctor and a fallen-away Catholic like me, who couldn't remember the last time I had prayed with other Christians, it was a powerful reminder that God is the one who gives dignity to both mother and baby, no matter the circumstance, and his Holy Spirit changes hearts and minds.

Their fervent dedication to supporting mothers and saving the lives of unborn children was inspiring, but I wondered if they would understand the tough spot I was in as a resident OB/GYN. What would they think if they knew I was required to terminate pregnancies as part of my job?

"In your Son's precious and holy name, Amen," Maggie closed.

After the prayer, she invited me into her office for a quick meeting. Like the other staff members, Maggie instantly put me at ease with her warm and chatty personality.

She opened the conversation by telling me how thankful she was to know another OB/GYN in the community. "We have a doctor on our board of directors, but we can't afford to hire one to work here," Maggie said.

"I'm happy to help in any way I can," I assured her.

She told me her volunteer staff was well versed in counseling their patients when it came to issues of social and material needs or spirituality, but they needed training to learn more about the medical technicalities of abortion procedures as well as the prenatal and delivery process so they could answer any basic questions the women might have.

This was before the medicalization of pregnancy centers. Back then, in the late 1980s, pregnancy centers were just starting to get in-house ultrasound machines and offer services like STD testing. Often, their clients were from low-income communities, sometimes even homeless, and hadn't received routine medical care in years. Expanding their medical capabilities was a priority for Maggie.

"Where does your funding come from?" I asked.

"Church donations, mostly," Maggie replied. She explained that she and many of the volunteers attended First Assembly of God, an evangelical church down the road. Their pastor, who was openly pro-life, had made it a point to encourage the people in the church to give to the pregnancy center. Their church was their biggest donor. "But it's a challenge to raise money, because a lot of pastors around here don't want to get into the pro-life/pro-choice debate."

She explained that their work was both biblically and scientifically based, pointing out that a baby's heartbeat can be detected as early as 18 to 21 days after fertilization. She figured many pastors just didn't want to touch the issue for fear of alienating some of their congregants. But she was determined to convince more churches in the community to get on board with their mission.

It was then that I realized just how radically pro-life she and her pregnancy center were. I had picked up on the fact that this was a pro-life center when I first dropped in, but hearing them express what was in their hearts during the prayer and speaking more with Maggie made me realize just how deep their convictions ran and also how politicized the nature of their work could be in a post–*Roe v. Wade* America.

But regardless of the political side of things, I felt a call to help these women and the women coming through their doors.

Just then, a young lady popped into the office. "Maggie, your six o'clock appointment is here."

She thanked the volunteer and turned to me. "Would you like to see what a client visit is like?"

"Absolutely," I said.

We met a young woman in the lobby who was in for her first appointment to confirm pregnancy. She had come in with a little boy no older than two. We introduced ourselves and showed her to the appointment room. Maggie began the intake process by asking her some basic questions to get to know her and why she had come in that day.

Through a thick Spanish accent, the young woman told us that she thought she was pregnant, but she didn't have health insurance and didn't know who to go to or what to do. She asked for a pregnancy test.

Maggie gently explained their process for confirming pregnancy with a urine test and a referral to a doctor's office for an ultrasound. She assured the woman they could help her if she was expecting and needed financial help, and not to worry. She handed her some information on local social services and told her the pregnancy center volunteers would help her navigate the process to make sure she got all of the help she needed, whether it was housing assistance or transportation to her prenatal appointments. She remained positive and hopeful throughout the conversation while also listening with compassion to her client's concerns.

I deeply appreciated that the pregnancy center helped their clients get whatever help they needed to support them in their pregnancy, whether it was maternity clothes and diapers or help navigating outside social services like counseling or housing or addiction treatment. At the hospital, we didn't offer women this kind of personal support. We gave some of our patients a referral

list of names and numbers they could call for social services, but there was not much follow-up to make sure
they received what they needed. Abortion seemed to
be treated as the all-encompassing answer to a woman's
pregnancy problem.

As they closed their meeting, Maggie asked her client
if she could pray with her. The client nodded yes as she
wiped away a tear that I sensed came from a relieved gratitude, and we all bowed our heads.

Supporting women at the pregnancy center in a way
that could save their unborn babies seemed like a noble
cause and a refreshing change of mindset from my residency. I was all in. From that day forward, I visited the
pregnancy center often. I advised Maggie and spoke to her
staff about fetal development to help them better guide
their clients in the beginning stages of pregnancy. She and
the volunteers became some of my closest friends in Norfolk and ended up teaching me much more than I felt I
had taught them. They helped me understand all the reasons women choose abortions and how to offer hope to
the hopeless. The love and care and compassion I found
in the pregnancy center staff was something I had never
seen in my residency colleagues. I became more curious
about the source of their joy, and it wasn't long before I
discovered it for myself.

I had never been to an evangelical service before, but I figured if the people at First Assembly of God were anything
like Maggie and the pregnancy center staff, they were people I wanted to be around. So I went without hesitation
when Maggie invited me to join her for worship.

When I arrived, I was struck by the architecture of the
church building—or lack thereof. It looked more like a
converted warehouse than a church. There was no steeple,

no bell, no stained glass. Rather than rows of wooden pews, the seating was theater-style, with cushy chairs that curved around in a semicircle. In the front there was no altar but a big stage and big speakers mounted on the wall on either side.

The church was packed with people, singles and families with children greeting one another and mingling. I was pleasantly surprised that several of them took notice of me, that I was a visitor, and introduced themselves. The people at First Assembly of God were some of the friendliest and most inviting I'd met during my time in Norfolk.

The lights went low. A man walked on stage with a guitar and started strumming chords as people hurried to find their seats. I spotted Maggie and her friends from across the room and grabbed a spot in her row.

The music was modern and uplifting with a contemporary feel. I thought of my organist father, who would have turned up his nose at this kind of music in a church. I chuckled to myself, wondering what he'd think if he knew I was here. Or maybe he would just be happy I was inside a church at all.

I didn't know any of the songs they sang, but the lyrics were displayed on a projector screen so I could sing along. We sang a song called "Open the Eyes of My Heart, Lord". I raised my hands along with Maggie and everyone else, closed my eyes, and allowed the lyrics to wash over me. In between tunes, the guitarist spoke about his journey with Christ. He said we had been bought with a price—forgiven, redeemed, and saved by faith in Jesus, and not by works. He encouraged the audience not only to sing with him but to share the only source of joy and truth, Jesus Christ, with others.

Nearly everything about this worship service was different from the traditional Catholicism I knew growing up. Though there was a rhythm to the evening, there was no official liturgy. People raised their hands, clapped, and sometimes danced whenever they felt moved. The mood in the church was electric, yet peaceful. These differences didn't matter to me at that moment. I enjoyed the freedom of it all.

In a strange way, it felt like the first time I had experienced true communion with God and his family. God was reaching me through the people at this evangelical church. It was exactly what I needed at that time.

The pastor closed in prayer on stage as the guitarist continued to play quietly in the background. He called the people to repentance and asked God to move the hearts of those who didn't know him.

I thought I knew God, but did I really know him in the way Maggie did? In the way the other people at the church did? Faith in Jesus was not a *part* of Maggie and the volunteers at the pregnancy center—it was their entire life. They knew they were forgiven and saved and filled with his love, and they were moved to share that love with others. I admitted to myself that I wasn't on fire for God in the same way they were. In fact, I was spiritually shipwrecked, and I knew it.

I closed my eyes and prayed the lyrics to "Open the Eyes of My Heart, Lord" in my own words. I asked God to help me with my unsettled conscience and to rescue me from myself. Even though I was surrounded by several hundred people, I was in the dark and alone with God.

I hummed the worship melodies to myself long after I left First Assembly of God that evening. I went home with a new joy for life and feeling oddly connected to hundreds of Christians I didn't know personally. I felt as if I had rediscovered Christ that night and my wandering heart was beginning to return to him.

Though the evening was full of joy for me, it also led to pain as I spent more time examining my conscience. I began to wrestle with the fact that I was living a double life: performing abortions during the day and advising the director at a pro-life pregnancy center at night. A real-life Dr. Jekyll and Mr. Hyde story. If what I was doing as an OB/GYN was really as brutal as I feared it was, how could God love someone like me? My heart and head were in a fierce battle. On one side, my head told me I was doing nothing wrong at the hospital. I was doing my job the way I had been taught in medical school. On the other side, my heart feared I had been willfully participating in violent acts against my patients: human babies in their most physically vulnerable state and their mothers in some of the most emotionally vulnerable moments of their lives.

I could feel God's love for me, and I knew he was drawing me in, closer and closer to his heart. And yet, with each passing day, the contrast between work I was doing at the hospital and the work I was doing at the pregnancy center became starker and more disturbing. Something had to change, and I knew it.

8

Full of Grace

I continued to live a double life, unsure how to solve the internal tension eating away at me. All of my inconsistencies finally came to a head that fateful night in labor and delivery at Norfolk General Hospital when I delivered the baby weighing just over 500 grams.

After I left the operating room, I wandered the hallways for a few moments to clear my head. The events of that morning repeated like an infinitely looping film reel inside my head. My patient telling me she "wanted it out". That her partner did not support her. Her fear of the high medical bills associated with a complicated pregnancy. My going along with her desires to end her pregnancy and breezing through important patient history questions. Her detached disposition. The lack of eye contact. Delivery. The scale's numerals flashing: 505 grams [17.8 ounces]. Hitting the emergency button. The disappointment on Dr. Plumb's face when she arrived. The transition team wheeling a tiny gasping baby out of the room. Dr. Plumb's burning words, which would remain seared in my memory for the rest of my life: *Stop giving me tumors, John. You're better than that.*

The whole event was confusing to me. I realized I had skipped over some questions on her medical history, but only because I was focused on what was more important: giving my patient what she wanted, what she had directly requested—an abortion. Had I pushed for more detail, I *might* have procured a more accurate understanding of the true progress of her pregnancy.

But the way I saw it, giving my patient what she said she needed was the best form of care I could offer her. I valued my reputation as a competent OB/GYN resident, and I was not accustomed to having my judgment—or my patient's, for that matter—brought into question. My professors had always praised my clinical insights for their clarity and thoroughness.

Good medicine, to me, meant the patient was always right, and therefore, as her physician, I needed to subordinate my feelings to hers. I had done exactly that. But Dr. Plumb's comments completely upended the way I viewed good medicine, and it rattled me.

And yet, being five grams "off" was nothing more than a technicality, the sort of error that could come from an improper zeroing of the scale. *What was the big deal?* If I had fudged the numbers, none of that would have happened, and frankly, no one would have even cared. Well, except Dr. Plumb.

I knew I was a good doctor. I'd worked diligently, studying the human body and the biological processes unique to women. I was confident in my knowledge. I could scientifically defend the viability of a fetus with statistics to back me up. I began to realize, however, that Dr. Plumb viewed the fetus from a completely different angle, through the lens of its humanity.

Suddenly, the very framework of my care for my patients came under attack. I assured myself that the decision to deliver the unwanted fetus had simply been one of benign neglect. *It was a tough case,* I told myself, *but I did the right thing by respecting this woman's will in the midst of a medically complicated situation. Didn't I?*

The accusation Dr. Plumb had leveled at me for my judgment swirled around my mind, taking root where my best defenses had once stood firm. *Was I cavalier in assuming the unborn fetus lacked the potential, even the will, to survive?* I began to wonder if, deep down, my whole mentality about medicine was gravely flawed, even evil. I shuddered at the thought.

My heart and head were being yanked in opposite directions. On one side was the OB/GYN resident determined to save the life of his patient's unborn child, and on the other was the same doctor treating a living human fetus like a cancerous tumor to be extracted and discarded. Dr. Plumb's words continued to haunt me. *Stop giving me tumors, John. You're better than that.*

It was late in the afternoon, and I realized I had forgotten to eat lunch again. I walked toward the doctor's lounge, hoping to find a sandwich from the drug company–sponsored lunch earlier that day, an optional event for residents that I now wished I had attended. I peeked inside to find only empty boxes stuffed in the garbage can. I was too late for leftovers.

I had just a few more minutes to clear this from my mind before seeing my next patient. So far I wasn't feeling any better about what had happened that morning.

On my way back to the clinic, I passed the hallway connecting Norfolk General Hospital with the Children's Hospital of the King's Daughters. The children's hospital boasted a level-three nursery, which allowed the NICU to care for very small and very sick babies under 32 weeks' gestational age. The neonatologists had the technology for ventilation and provided expert care for babies delivered as early as 23 weeks, which in 1989, was remarkable. Their team specialized in treating immature fetal lungs and had great success in caring for babies on the borderline of viability. I wondered if the experts in the NICU had been, by some miracle, able to resuscitate the 505-gram [17.8 ounce] fetus I had delivered alive just hours earlier. But I knew the likelihood of survival was slim.

Just then, my stomach dropped. Dr. Deborah Plumb was walking toward me. I was still feeling humiliated from the incident earlier that morning. The last thing I wanted was to run into her again that day, but the encounter was unavoidable.

"Hi, John." Her face was unreadable as she stopped in front of me. "Do you have time to grab coffee tomorrow?"

I could hear my heart beating in my temples. Seeing Dr. Plumb was enough to stir up a fear that my professors might think less of me after that morning. I knew Dr. Plumb wanted to talk more about what had happened earlier, but I was dreading having to revisit the details. And didn't she know how busy I was? Between clinical rotations, lectures, and deliveries, I was barely squeezing in enough sleep, let alone making time to chat. I just wanted to forget the whole event and erase it from my memory as soon as possible. I figured I didn't have much of a choice, though, and reluctantly agreed to the coffee appointment. We decided on seven thirty the next morning in the café downstairs.

As she walked away, that pang in my gut returned, reminding me of my hunger. I turned to the vending machine on the other side of the hallway, pushed two quarters into the coin slot, and watched the plastic spiral unwind to release a candy bar—a quick and easy fuel fix before I returned to the clinic.

The café was on the first floor, a warmly lit area with four cushioned chairs around each table and the smell of good cooking, more like a bistro than a hospital cafeteria. As I entered the restaurant the next morning, I saw Dr. Plumb sitting at a table in her white coat, a steaming cup of coffee in front of her. I quickly poured myself a cup of dark roast at the counter and walked toward the table, bracing myself for an awkward conversation. I pulled out the chair across from her and sat down. "Good morning, Dr. Plumb," I said through a forced smile. After we had exchanged small talk, to my surprise, she began to compliment me.

"John, I think you're going to be a great doctor. I see how compassionate you are and how well you listen to your patients." She went on to say that she cared about my development as a doctor and noticed that I strove to care for "the whole person"—the mind, body, and soul of every patient. "You'll make a great obstetrician. *But*, what happened yesterday—I just think you're better than that."

"Yeah, I apologize. I should have handled it differently . . ."

She shook her head. "It's more than that, John. These severely premature infants are my patients. In order for me to care for *my* patient to the best of my ability, you have to give me the healthiest baby possible, so I can take care of him afterwards. It makes no sense to extract the baby like a tumor just prior to birth and then expect me to care for him in that condition after delivery. When you ignore these babies, it makes my job so much more difficult."

Again, her words stopped me in my tracks. I thought of the baby that had slid into my palms, terribly bruised from a less-than-delicate birth experience. I thought of the massive effort on the part of the neonatal team to resuscitate a tiny child I had just minutes before agreed to abort. Disappointment washed over me as the realization penetrated my calloused heart that I'd provided an abortion service for my patient just because she'd asked, not because it had been the best medical option for her or her child.

In the midst of this sinking realization, Dr. Plumb spoke to my battered heart and challenged me, repeating her words from yesterday. "You care for more than one patient in the delivery room, John. Mother *and* baby."

Though Dr. Plumb was disappointed in my handling of the situation, she showed nothing but compassion toward me. Her genuine care for me, coupled with the piercing truth of her words, rearranged everything I'd believed about practicing good medicine.

When I look back, it is as if the Lord were throwing me a life preserver in the form of Dr. Plumb. The barrage of confusion I'd been experiencing since the delivery subsided, and a peace washed over me that I hadn't felt in a long time. Still, I couldn't have known that God was using this conversation to begin chiseling at my hardened heart in a way that would change my entire life.

Dr. Plumb must have sensed something changing in me. "Have you ever thought about going to Medjugorje?"

Majoo-what? I wondered. I had no idea what this had to do with our conversation. "No, where's that?"

Dr. Plumb described her recent trip to a village in Yugoslavia called Medjugorje. She referred to her trip as a "pilgrimage" and said she'd gone there with a Christian university for prayer and reflection. I must have mentioned to her in passing that I went to church. Perhaps that was why she felt comfortable sharing her spiritual experience with me.

Dr. Plumb said the trip to Medjugorje had changed her life, especially how she viewed her calling to practice good medicine. She suggested that traveling to this remote village might give me a better perspective on my calling as well. Perhaps the experience would help me think through the importance of caring for both mother and child as dignified, individual persons, both made in the image of God.

Dr. Plumb seemed to have that concept figured out, and I was beginning to realize just how far I was from understanding what practicing good medicine truly meant.

I was unaware of it, but the town of Medjugorje had become somewhat famous eight years earlier when news spread of a group of children who claimed the Virgin Mary was appearing to them on a hilltop and encouraging them to pray and have faith. Dr. Plumb explained to me that since the visions were reported, Medjugorje had become a place of deep prayer, quiet reflection, and commitment or recommitment to Christ for those who travel there. After visiting the village, many people claimed to feel closer to God and felt convicted to live a better life, to bear fruit in response to Christ's grace. Some people even claimed Mary or Jesus appeared to them on the hilltop as well.

Though apparently the town had a rather spiritual reputation, I still found Dr. Plumb's suggestion odd. I had never heard of Medjugorje. I couldn't even pronounce it properly. At first, I wondered if "Medjugorje" was more of a spiritual state of mind than an actual spot on the map. When I realized she was talking about a real place, I was still unclear about how a trip to a small village in Eastern Europe might offer insight into the medical field. We were trained physicians, pledged to the schools of scientific data and proven methodology. *The only thing "medical" about Medjugorje*, I chuckled to myself, *is the medical examinations these "visionaries" need.* It sounded like a bunch of baloney to me.

Another reason her suggestion didn't initially resonate with me was that Mary seemed to be the one front and center in her story, not Jesus. This was one of my major hang-ups with my abandoned Catholic roots. Despite my experience at the church in Mexico City back in medical school, I agreed with my friends from the Assembly of God church I occasionally attended in Virginia Beach: focusing on Mary too much was a distraction from Christ. I considered Marian worship a theological heresy. (I later learned that Catholics do too.) I didn't see how a trip to a village on the other side of the world—a village made famous by an alleged appearance of Mary and currently caught in the middle of Soviet strife, no less!—warranted my serious consideration.

At that time in my life, I resisted many things I had learned in Catholic school and Confirmation class growing up. Yet part of me was still affected by the way my parents spoke about the mother of Jesus. Dad taught me that Mary's Yes to the angel's invitation to become the Mother of God undid the curse of Eve. In the Garden, Eve ushered sin into the world when she chose to disobey God's command not to eat from the Tree of Knowledge of Good and Evil. But in a stunning reversal of the curse, God chose to usher salvation into the world through another woman—through Mary, whose willing obedience to the Lord made her the vessel through which Christ came to pay the penalty for sin. I thought about the Hail Marys we'd prayed together as a family every morning before school, from the words spoken by the Angel Gabriel in Luke 1:28: "Hail ... the Lord is with thee: blessed art thou among women" (King James version). Dad would lead us through one decade of the Rosary, asking Mary to pray for us. While I didn't accept the way most Catholics I knew appeared to worship Mary, hearing Dr. Plumb tell the story of Medjugorje seemed to uncover a long-lost yearning to understand Mary's role and how she might lead me closer to Christ.

"You should just check it out. You might be surprised."

Though I still wasn't planning on taking her pilgrimage advice, I was thankful for our conversation and her courage in challenging my thinking about caring for two patients instead of just one.

I was weary of living a double life, with one foot in the pregnancy center and one foot in the hospital performing abortions on demand. I was tired of altering my approach to patients according to how much the mother seemed to want to continue her pregnancy.

I thanked Dr. Plumb for her time. I knew I was done giving her "tumors" instead of patients, but I didn't ask her what had happened to the 505-gram [17.8 ounce] baby.

At the time, I couldn't imagine that Dr. Plumb's suggestion would actually send me on a trip halfway across the world and forever change the course of my life. I left our coffee conversation unprepared for the work God still had left to do on my soul. But he made his intentions clear through a plan Mom proposed only days later.

As I always did after a long day at the hospital, I walked the quarter mile up Colley Avenue to my studio apartment, kicked off my shoes at the door, and collapsed on my mattress on the floor. In an attempt to force my mind away from my patients and hospital work, I focused on the ridges and valleys of my stucco ceiling.

The residents' daily grind of 6 A.M. patient rounds, then lectures, clinical appointments, surgeries, and deliveries, had me running on empty, physically and spiritually. Every third or fourth day we were on call, and our on-call "days" lasted 36 hours. We caught sleep wherever we could. After a day and a half of work, we'd finally go home for a meal, a shower, and a chance to catch up on sleep before doing it all over again in 12 hours. Our winter break was coming, and boy, could I use it.

When my mind calmed and I had gathered the energy to sit up, I reached over to my phone and dialed home.

The pigtail phone cord allowed me just enough slack to reach my studio kitchen to microwave some taco-seasoned ground beef while the phone rang. Speaking with Mom was the most comforting half hour of my week. It helped me decompress from the fast-paced atmosphere of the hospital.

Mom was very attentive and loved to talk about easy topics: recent meals she'd made, such as split-pea and ham hock soup—one of Dad's favorites—how winter weather had come to Mahwah and Norfolk, and trips she wanted to take around the world. That day, she jumped right into her favorite subject. "Johnny, what are you doing for winter break?"

I heard a spark of excitement in her voice, and I knew what that meant: Mom was going to pitch an idea for our next adventure together. She knew that she'd given me the travel bug and that I wouldn't pass up a trip with her. And she was right. I had loved traveling with Mom ever since we drove up and down the East Coast together to tour medical schools.

I told her I didn't have any plans.

"Want to go to Medjugorje?"

9

Medjugorje

Mom gazed out the window as I slid her black suitcase into the plane's overhead compartment and sat down next to her. She was in a chatty mood, and I could tell she was excited about our next adventure.

We were on our way to Dubrovnik, Croatia, on the Mediterranean, and then to Medjugorje, the Yugoslavian village where many people believe the Virgin Mary has been appearing. In 1981 six children claimed that a beautiful woman holding an infant had appeared to them seven days in a row with messages about peace, faith, conversion, fasting, and prayer. The seers said the lady told them she was the Blessed Virgin Mary, but the Holy See has not authenticated the visions.

While Mom admitted she wasn't certain about the story, what really struck her was the response from people all around the world who had been swarming to the tiny village ever since. For many, it was a religious pilgrimage; others came out of curiosity or a desire for adventure. Pilgrims and tourists reported many stories of faith conversions during their visit—people coming to know Christ for the first time or rediscovering him and deepening their walk with him. Mom knew I had fallen away from the Catholic Church and was only occasionally attending services at the Assembly of God church in Norfolk. I suspected that she was hoping this trip would reignite my Catholic faith. I knew she prayed a Rosary for me every day, that I would return to the Church. Spending time with her was my primary reason for going. Every moment with Mom was precious because I knew she loved me, warts and all.

I was trying to be as excited about the spiritual aspect as I knew Mom was, but I was feeling empty and worn out to the core. Work at the hospital was exhausting, though my fatigue felt different this time. Heavier. It pulled on every part of my body, but mostly my soul. The tension of living a morally erratic life was becoming more obvious to me. I looked forward to escaping this "schizophrenic" tug-of-war within me and the stress of residency, if only momentarily. Perhaps spending time in prayer on this pilgrimage would help ease that tension and calm my anxiety.

The rumble of the plane engines grew louder. The runway lines dashed past my window, each one faster than the next. After we left the ground, I closed my eyes and drifted off into a peaceful doze, leaving my troubles in America.

Dusk approached as our bus reached our accommodations in Medjugorje. As we collected our luggage, a local woman snuck up behind Mom and grabbed her shoulder. Mom jumped and held onto me in reaction. Startled, we both looked at the woman, with her tousled hair and rumpled clothing.

"Look up! Look up!" she shrieked. Her eyes looked wild, and her mostly toothless grin even wilder. She pointed to the sky. "See the way the sun dances?"

We looked up at the sun that hung low over a small mountain in the distance, thinking this woman must be deranged. Then she took a step closer to me, close enough to grab me by the collar. "Your life is going to be changed here!" she howled. Then she scurried away as suddenly as she had appeared.

If this encounter was the appetizer of our trip to Medjugorje, I questioned whether I really wanted the entrée. I hoped the incident was not a bad omen, foreshadowing four days of hanging out with kooky villagers who claimed to see visions of Mary and Jesus. What had we signed ourselves up for? I tried to remain open-minded to the experience ahead of me.

We arrived at a little home near a church in town where we would stay for the next three nights. A petite gray-haired Herzegovinian woman greeted us at the front door. "*Bok, dobrodošli!* Come in, come in!" she said as she shuffled us inside. She quickly hung up our coats and showed us our rooms. Though the winter sun had set and we were tired from a full day of travel, Mom suggested we catch the evening Mass at Saint James Catholic Church down the block.

The next morning, our host served us bread with cheese and baloney for breakfast. Mom and I thanked her and set out to hike Cross Mountain. This mount was not the hilltop where the child visionaries claimed Mary had revealed herself to them, but the tallest peak in Medjugorje (about 1,700 feet) and only about a two-mile walk west from Apparition Hill. A concrete cross had been constructed at the top of Cross Mountain by the townspeople in 1934 to commemorate 1,900 years since the death of Jesus.

We ventured through the tiny village that sat between hills connected by sheep trails and patches of olive trees. We passed by old cottages and crumbling farmhouses with thatched roofs in the center of town. Newer concrete duplexes around the old town had sprung up in recent years to accommodate the pilgrims. Townspeople sold rosaries and other religious trinkets to the pilgrims and tourists.

When we reached the foot of Cross Mountain, we noticed that the path up was steep and rocky. "Do you think I can do this?" Mom asked.

"Of course you can, Mom," I said. The truth was, I was worried it would be hard on her asthma, and she had not brought her inhaler with her. But I knew nothing could stop Mom from a good adventure. I assured her we'd take as many breaks as she needed.

The rocky zigzag path was marked with 14 large brass reliefs of the Stations of the Cross. We stopped at each image depicting events from Christ's Passion, from when he is condemned to death before Pontius Pilate to when his body is buried in the tomb. The Stations brought me back to my childhood, when we'd pray before similar images at our church in Mahwah on Good Friday—and they provided the hiking breaks Mom needed.

When we reached the top of the mountain, I looked over at my Mom and smiled at her, proud that she had made it up the hill without her puffer. We found flat rocks to sit on to soak in the beauty of the nearly 30-foot cross towering over us. The January wind rushed around me, creating a calming white noise. The world stretched out behind the cross in a patchwork of farmland below. Being nearer to the clouds helped me feel closer to God, even if I wasn't fully open to his will for my life at the moment.

On my rock, I prayed and read Scripture. I jotted down rambling thoughts in my journal about why I was there—to be with Mom—and why I thought God had called me to be a doctor. Even though I thought that being a doctor was a noble calling and that the healing power of medicine and a doctor's touch symbolized God's mercy as the Great Physician, I wasn't sure why God had called me specifically to a physician's line of work. It was a question I hadn't spent much time thinking about until I was in Medjugorje, and a question for which I didn't yet have an answer.

I thought about how medical technology was pushing the limits of life by aborting life, preventing life, and freezing life. Doctors are given life-changing and even eternity-changing power. Maybe my job was not only to ensure well-being based on a list of medical pros and cons. Maybe it was larger than that. Deeper than that.

Later that evening, after the sun had set, Mom and I attended Mass down the street from our host family's house. We met another American there, Camille. She was a young woman from Baltimore who was living and working in Medjugorje to discern whether or not to become a nun. She invited Mom and me to walk up Apparition Hill, the site of the reported visions, to pray. Camille enjoyed praying outside at night because it was what Jesus did in the Garden of Gethsemane. Mom was exhausted after a long day of hiking and exploring the town, so she declined the invitation, but I felt God nudging me to make the pilgrim's trek up the mountain.

The moon lit our walk toward the base of the hill. I thought back to the woman we had met the prior evening who told me my life was going to change here and the eerie feeling she left with me. Though Medjugorje seemed like a pleasant place, with generous villagers opening their homes and offering homemade food and drinks to the pilgrims, I still felt a dark energy in the town— especially as Camille and I marched toward the hill to pray that evening.

Just as we reached the base of the mountain, a startling howl shattered the midnight silence. It sounded both beastly and human, very different from the wails of birth pangs and other kinds of intense physical pain. Out of the forest galloped what looked like a man on all fours. I could not believe my eyes. What *is* this?

I stood frozen and regretted not bringing a flashlight. Camille stayed calm, as the dark, growling figure ran off. Then she looked at me and said, "Let's keep going."

We began our hike up the mountain. On the way, she explained what she thought we had heard and seen. There had been several reports of demonic activity in the town: people writhing on the ground, foaming at the mouth, screaming and shouting angrily and uncontrollably in foreign tongues during Mass. While the priests in the town believed some of these incidents had strictly medical or psychological explanations, they said many were demonic possessions requiring exorcism. People from far and wide came to Medjugorje for healing, and I suppose I did, too. I still had unrepented sin and deep-rooted shame and guilt that were growing in my heart like weeds among the grain.

When we reached the top, Camille knelt on a rock and began reciting psalms from memory. I walked a few yards away to pray silently by myself. I prayed for whatever the midnight yowling meant—for whatever pain that man must have been feeling to utter such a heart-wrenching sound. I prayed for his body and soul and contemplated the connection between physical illness and sin.

I was no better off than that man. Spiritual warfare was raging in my heart and had been for a long time. Racing thoughts about the state of my soul flooded my mind. I asked God, *Why don't I feel at peace? What is wrong with me?* I confessed that I doubted his love for me and pleaded for answers. It was the first time I remember praying *for* myself in a long time.

Through silence, God revealed all the garbage in my heart and mind. I was attached to things of this world:

MEDJUGORJE 135

respect in my field, approval from my peers and patients, and science that left no room for mystery. I elevated the things of the world that were observable over the things that I knew were real but more difficult to study objectively, such as the love between mother and child, husband and wife, God and sinner.

The darkness weighed on me. Memories of patients flashed through my mind, especially the cases that ended in violence and created tension in my heart. I acknowledged the conflict and chaos inside my soul and that I was unhappy. I was a man, a doctor, a son in need of help.

I fought my exhaustion and continued to pray for my soul, thinking about Jesus in the Garden praying under the moonlight in agony while his disciples slept. Now was not the time to give in to fatigue.

This was a whole-body prayer that I felt in every cell and pore. Sweat collected across my forehead. I felt the Holy Spirit praying for me. I felt Christ entering into the suffering of my sins and the sins of the whole world from the beginning to the end. I felt the loving embrace of a Father.

When we were both finished praying, I rejoined Camille in the darkness.

"Where Jesus is at work, so is evil," she said. "But the fruits of this place are phenomenal and available to those who ask."

The next morning, Mom and I hiked up Apparition Hill together. She was relieved the trek to the top would be a shorter distance than the one up Cross Mountain.

The trailhead was at the end of a dirt road in the village between farm houses and dilapidated lean-tos that provided shade for animals. Church groups sang worship songs on their hike up the stony path to the top. Some prayed the Rosary aloud in unison. People carried sick family members or friends up the hill on stretchers in hopes of a miracle. Pilgrims walked up barefoot as an act of penance. We saw visitors of every age, especially youths. I felt a sense of peace as we climbed closer to the top.

Visitors were standing and kneeling all over the rocky summit. A few candles were set at the foot of the cross, and prayer notes penned by pilgrims were scattered all around in the nooks and crannies of the rocks. Mom went her way and I went mine, searching for a flat rock to kneel on and pray in solitude. I was alone.

Suddenly, I got the sense that something was very wrong with my body, and I began to feel very sick. I felt a strange sensation all over my skin, as if it were infected, scabbing, and scaly. I searched my forearms for a rash or blisters, but my skin looked normal and healthy.

I then realized that the physical sensations were revealing a spiritual reality, that inside I was a leper—unclean, covered with painful lesions. I was confused and frightened. I pleaded with God to stop the torment and pain. I asked to know him with the eyes of my heart as Abba, Father, not an intellectual abstraction ... if he was there.

What happened next is nearly indescribable. I saw an image of a man standing in front of me wearing a white robe, with wounds on his hands and feet. I got the sense that I was on holy ground and that Jesus had invited me here. He was seeking *me*. But in an instant, the image disappeared, as quickly as an afterimage fades when you look at a bright light and then close your eyes.

I was startled but calm. I looked around to see if anyone else had seen what I had seen, but no one was looking in my direction. Everyone continued on as normal. The experience felt similar to the time I heard a voice speak to me at the Basilica of Our Lady of Guadalupe in Mexico City, in that I struggled to distinguish whether what I was seeing, hearing, and feeling was reality or my imagination.

He had been right there in front of me, so real, and yet how could this be?

Just then, a woman walked up to me unexpectedly. She introduced herself and said that she was here with a Belgian pro-life group. "Are you from America?" she asked.

Still rattled from thinking I had just seen Jesus, I was taken off guard. "Yes ...," I replied hesitantly, wondering where this conversation might lead.

"Are you a doctor?" she asked.

"Yes, I am. How did you know that?"

"Crazy things happen here," she said, chuckling. "I was just praying for you, and Mary told me several things about you that I need to pass on. Are you open to hearing it?"

"Um, no, sorry. I don't think I'm open to it right now." I was still feeling ill and just wanted to be alone.

"Well, it's your choice." She looked at me, waiting to see if I'd reconsider.

I gave in. "OK. I guess it can't hurt to listen."

"The message is that God loves you and desires you for himself. He died for you, he died for me, he died for his mother. We didn't deserve it or earn it. Jesus died in your place because he loves you, and he's inviting you to walk with him. Mary just wants us to follow her Son and to do whatever he tells us to do."

She continued on, explaining the Gospel and speaking to me in a way that reached deep inside my soul. What she said next shook me to my core. "Mary said three things: to be the best doctor you can be, always to see the poor and see them daily, and to follow the teachings of her Son's Church."

Is this woman a visionary or a messenger from God? How could she have known to say all the right things that I needed to hear? I wondered. I felt that she was delivering a special message from God, directly to me. I jotted everything down in my journal as she was saying it.

I wanted to be the doctor God wanted me to be, but I knew I hadn't been. My heart had been hardened. With every abortion I had participated in, my heart had calcified a little bit more.

"I don't know why you're here or who you are; I just know I had to tell you this," she said.

Her words filled me with peace. I thanked her, and before I knew it, she left, walking back the way she came. I placed my journal down at my feet and immediately knelt again in prayer to talk to God about my strange experience and the message this woman had delivered to me.

Then the man in the white robe appeared again. *Is this really Jesus?* I didn't understand how I was seeing what I was seeing. It was as if I could reach out and touch him. Then he spoke to me. He told me that he loved me and asked me if I wanted to be healed.

I still felt viscerally ill. I felt undeserving in every sense, unworthy to be in his presence. He loved me, but I realized how little I had loved him in return. How little I loved others as he loved me. Tears ran down my cheeks and fell to the ground. "You know I want to be healed, Lord," I answered.

At that moment, my whole life flashed before my eyes. I saw a snapshot reel of my past sins. Gluttony in filling myself with pleasures of the world and approval of man. Pride to be above question and reproach in my job, as a doctor with life and death under my thumb. The violence I committed under the guise of professionalism. My hands on Dr. Rose's hands as we ended the life of a human baby in the safety of his mother's womb. Then another abortion. And another. The blood of those tiny ones on my hands. My heart's callous response to the baby weighing 505 grams [17.8 ounces], just big enough to require medical intervention. So many moments rushed through my mind, I could barely keep track of them—each one contributing to a final verdict: diseased by sin.

Yet Christ showed me how he loved me all along the way, even in the pits of my ugliest, most violent sins. I felt unworthy, but his love engulfed my shame.

Next, a beautiful woman who I believe was Mary stepped forward. She told me that her Son had come to renew the face of the earth. He makes all things new, she assured me.

She gave me specific instructions, the same ones the Belgian woman had given me: first, to be the best doctor I could be and to practice excellent medicine; second, to see the underserved and to see them daily; and third, to follow the teachings of her Son's Church.

She said that the temptations to disobey these instructions would be great but that her Son would never let me down or leave me.

"Will you trust his love for you?" she asked.

"I will. I do."

And it all began to make sense: the evils of life-destroying medical practices, the universal truth of natural law and Church teaching, and the love of Jesus Christ.

Suddenly, the leprous feeling disappeared and my skin came back to life. The scales fell from my eyes. The weight of sin melted away. I had been healed by the Great Physician. I felt loved, redeemed, and brand new.

As quickly as the figures had appeared, they were gone. I couldn't believe how vivid my conversation with Jesus and his mother had seemed. Nothing like that had ever happened to me before. The only thing I could compare it to was the voice I thought I had heard in Mexico City and ignored. I now knew that moment was a precious gift that I had wasted.

I practically flew down Apparition Hill, hopping from rock to rock, feeling full of life and joy. I thanked God for revealing himself to me and loving me, a leper. I immediately went to Saint James Catholic Church and confessed my sins aloud to a priest for the first time in a decade: the abortions and bad principles I had adhered to all these years. I was forgiven and free, redeemed by Christ.

The Lord changed my heart and life forever at Medjugorje. I know that my story might sound crazy and that some people might not believe it. If readers are skeptical, I understand and don't blame them. I don't know for sure why God chose to speak to me in such a strange and unbelievable way, but maybe he had to. My heart was so hard and my soul so entrenched in sin that I needed a radical encounter. I didn't come to Medjugorje seeking such a vivid spiritual experience, but that was how God chose to act in my life. The way in which he chose to reveal himself to me and speak to my heart was so transformational that I was like a dead man who had come back to life. I knew that the course of my future as a man, a physician, and a son of God had been changed forever.

Coming Home

1990

After returning from Medjugorje, I knew I had to tell the most important people in my life what kind of doctor I had been called to be: a doctor who heals instead of hurts. It sounds simple, but I had a feeling that putting this calling into practice would be more complicated.

Like the Prodigal Son, I had turned away from my Father, especially when it came to practicing medicine. But he scooped me up from the depth of my darkest sins on the hilltop in Medjugorje and offered me an unimaginable joy, a resurrection of sorts, known only by those willing to receive his undeserved love and forgiveness. God changed the vantage point from which I viewed life, eternity, and medicine. Now it was time for me to walk with him in obedience.

I had performed abortions for the first two years of my residency. I terminated Down syndrome babies. I terminated babies with deformities. I terminated babies whose conditions were "incompatible with life". From a medical standpoint, the problem with this "treatment" is that doctors are trying to get rid of the disease by getting rid of the people with the disease. Yet when doctors care for both patients, mother and child, they begin to view the "diseased" child as a person who is worthy of love. I wanted to be one of those doctors. A new paradigm began to form within my mind, and I could feel it invigorating a new passion for practicing truly excellent, God-honoring, and life-affirming medicine. Medicine, for me, would be an act of mercy, never again an act of violence.

I immersed myself in Catholic ethics and theology and began to read the Bible with fresh eyes. I had been inundated with too many different interpretations of Scripture concerning medical ethics by various pastors and Christian friends of various denominations in the past. I wanted one truth, one church, one bread.

Through my return to Catholic Church teaching, God showed me his design for creation. I learned that medicine should work with and not against the complex and beautifully synchronized systems of the body. I needed to see my patients as God's creation, fallen under sin but one day to be restored in full by Jesus. In the meantime, their health was to be handled delicately and honorably by cooperating with the physiological language of the body. From Tepeyac Hill and the rocky path in Medjugorje, God was showing me a better calling: *truly* to care for his image bearers. The heartbroken mother, the hurting father, the child in the womb unknown to this world and yet at the mercy of it, my fellow doctor—all image bearers of the good and gracious God, who had saved me from the hopelessness of sin. I would, with his help, treat whomever he brought to me as he had treated me: with the grace of a loving father toward his prodigal son.

God helped me sort through the scientific details by giving me a living role model to look up to—one of the most renowned genetic researchers in the history of medicine, French doctor Jérôme Lejeune. Dr. Lejeune had been a likely candidate for the Nobel Prize for his research into the genetic cause of Down syndrome. He also happened to be a believer, a Catholic man with a quick wit and a love for his patients. Dr. Lejeune was called to testify in an in vitro fertilization (IVF)–related court case that involved Eastern Virginia Medical School, where I was doing my residency.

The *Davis v. Davis* case gained public attention in the late 1980s and early 1990s. It was a dispute between a divorced couple over the fate of their embryos, who had been conceived in vitro and then frozen. The father, Junior Lewis Davis, wanted the right to destroy the embryos against his former wife's wishes. After suffering five ectopic pregnancies, Mary Sue Davis was no longer able to conceive naturally and wanted the option to implant the embryos and carry the children to term or to donate the embryos to a couple struggling to conceive. The court overseeing the couple's divorce determined the embryos to be "children in vitro", and the judge ruled in favor of the mother. The ruling said that the embryos, as human beings, had the right to be given a chance to grow to full term.[1] Given the very little legal precedent on which to base the decision, the case was taken to the Tennessee Court of Appeals and later brought before the Tennessee Supreme Court. Ultimately, the case was decided in favor of the father, who, said the courts, had a right not to become a parent against his will.[2] The case raised ethical questions over IVF and the big question of whether human life begins at the moment of fertilization.

The Davis embryos had been conceived in a lab by my residency program at Eastern Virginia Medical School

[1] Jennifer E. Chapman and Mark Zhang, "Davis v. Davis (1992)", The Embryo Project Encyclopedia, October 17, 2013, https://embryo.asu.edu /pages/davis-v-davis-1992.

[2] Chapman and Zhang, "Davis v. Davis".

(EVMS), headed by Dr. Howard Jones and his wife, Dr. Georgeanna Jones. They were world-renowned doctors from Johns Hopkins who founded the Jones Institute for Reproductive Medicine in the OB/GYN department at EVMS. The doctor couple were luminaries, founding pillars of modern obstetrics and gynecology. Dr. Howard was an expert corrective surgeon of uterine defects, and Dr. Georgeanna was an expert on hormones and reproductive physiology. After they retired from Johns Hopkins, they came to Norfolk, Virginia, to start the first and for a long time premier IVF center in the United States at EVMS.

The Jones Institute was on the cutting edge of IVF technology in the 1980s. Just a few years before I arrived as a resident, the institute had conceived the first IVF baby in the United States and the 15th in the entire world, Elizabeth Carr, born in 1981.[3] Everyone seemed to be buzzing over the limitless possibilities in this field, and I was excited to be learning from some of the greatest fertility doctors in the world.

During my second year of residency, I spent a few months studying under Dr. Georgeanna to help families have more babies like Elizabeth. I assisted in caring for IVF patients, studied cervical secretions that help a woman's body receive sperm to promote fertilization, assisted in the operating room during egg retrieval or embryo implantation, and learned about IVF innovation from the weekly round-table discussions among the top doctors and scientists in the Infertility Division.

First-, second-, and third-year residents watched egg retrieval behind the fellows and senior residents. Eggs

[3] Walter Sullivan, "'Test-Tube' Baby Born in U.S., Joining Successes around the World", *New York Times*, December 29, 1981, https://www.nytimes.com/1981/12/29/science/test-tube-baby-born-in-us-joining-successes-around-the.html.

would be graded for quality and likelihood of producing optimal embryos, whether they were immature, too mature, or just right. Dr. Georgeanna would clap her hands for the optimal eggs.

Caring for IVF patients was a rewarding and, in a sense, redeeming aspect of my job. Before Medjugorje, assisting life in this fashion seemed to balance out the downside of my profession—abortion. I was fascinated by the possibilities IVF could provide for women struggling to conceive. As with all my practice, I committed myself to doing IVF procedures with excellence.

One afternoon I sat in a darkened lecture hall at Sentara Norfolk General Hospital during Grand Rounds, an event for the local medical community where the entire department gathered to discuss important topics relevant to the field. Dr. Howard Jones spoke that day on the Davis case. He seemed to agree with the father that the embryos were property, not persons with their own rights and legal protections. He called them "pre-embryos". This term suggested an intermediate status to the medical community. It indicated an acceptable gray area that would allow for more medical experimentation. Pre-embryos, he argued, were more significant than, say, an appendix, but not to be given the dignity of human personhood.

Dr. Howard was an excellent physician with a brilliant mind, and he also happened to be God-fearing. I believe he understood that a unique human life was formed at fertilization. But I suspected he used the intermediate term "pre-embryo" to advance IVF research and the success rates at the Jones Institute. The term gave a nod to the embryo's *potential* dignity, but it also left room to study embryos in whatever way was necessary for the "greater good" of treating and helping women with infertility. He wanted to relieve the pain of wanting a child but being unable to conceive one or sustain a pregnancy, and he needed the freedom to produce, transfer, destroy, and freeze embryos to do it.

I studied the Davis case closely and initially agreed with my professor's position. But when I heard Dr. Lejeune argue in favor of embryonic personhood, I thought his perspective was more consistent and sounder. In April 1981, when asked by the U.S. Senate Judiciary Subcommittee, "When does human life begin?", this was his answer:

> At two months of age, the human being is less than one thumb's length from the head to the rump. He would fit at ease in a nutshell, but everything is there: hands, feet, head, organs, brain, all are in place. His heart has been beating for a month already. Looking closely, you would see the palm creases and a fortune teller would read the good adventure of that tiny person. With a good magnifier the fingerprints could be detected. Every document is available for a national identity card....
>
> Science has turned the fairytale of Tom Thumb into a true story, the one each of us has lived in the womb of his mother.
>
> And to let you measure how precise the detection can be: if at the beginning, just after conception, days before implantation, a single cell was removed from the little berry-looking individual, we could cultivate that cell and examine its chromosomes....
>
> To accept the fact that, after fertilization has taken place, a new human has come into being is no longer a matter of taste or of opinion. The human nature of the human being from conception to old age is not a metaphysical contention. It is plain experimental evidence.[4]

---

[4] John S. Hamlon, "Human Life in the Fast Lane: Conversing with Jérôme Lejeune", *The Catholic World Report*, December 15, 2021, https://www.catholicworldreport.com/2013/05/27/human-life-in-the-fast-lane-conversing-with-jerome-lejeune/.

Dr. Lejeune didn't usually quote Scripture in his testimonies, and he always delivered his case with incredible wit and a deep understanding of the truth to be discovered by science. Throughout his life he used clever phrases such as "In the beginning was the code, and the code was with God." Eventually, it clicked for me. The science and faith aspects of genetics and fertilization all came together as one truth.

Genetically, human embryos are human beings. They are not appendices or monkeys or house plants. They are part of the human family, tiny image bearers of the God who made them.

Through IVF, human embryos were being produced but not always implanted. Some were frozen, others discarded. But human embryos don't belong in a freezer or a trash can—they are children. And we have a responsibility to love these tiny children, the least of our brothers and sisters.

In 1992, the Tennessee Supreme Court ultimately ruled in favor of Mr. Davis, allowing his embryos to be destroyed according to the clinic's practices and setting a precedent favoring parents who wished to "avoid procreation".[5] Still, Dr. Lejeune was and remains my biggest influence for practicing my profession as a doctor in a way that is both morally and scientifically sound.

Having been brought to my senses in Yugoslavia, I nervously waited outside Dr. Georgeanna Jones' office, the center of my medical home. She was the most influential person in the entire OB/GYN department, so I decided to tell her first about my change of heart and be prepared for the consequences of my newfound insights.

[5] "Davis v. Davis", Justia US Law, accessed December 16, 2021, https://law.justia.com/cases/tennessee/supreme-court/1992/842-s-w-2d-588-2.html.

Dr. Georgeanna and I had a great relationship. Along with Dr. Rose, she was one of my greatest mentors during residency and almost like a wise grandmother figure to me. She had an outstanding scientific mind. She taught me to listen carefully to the signs of a woman's body, that something so easily dismissed as cervical mucus actually whispers indications of fertility. Dr. Georgeanna believed in me. She wanted me to succeed as a competent and compassionate doctor with respect for the marvelous workings of a patient's body.

We even occasionally talked about faith, which is how I learned that she and her husband were both Christians. But Dr. Georgeanna walked a fine line between the pro-life and pro-choice worlds. While I was hopeful she would understand my perspective, I still worried the news I was about to share would disappoint her.

She welcomed me into her office, and I took the seat across from her desk. I explained everything. I told her all about the 505-gram [17.8 ounce] baby and the change of heart that had come from my trip to Medjugorje. "I'm convinced that human life begins at fertilization and that every reproductive manipulation or destructive act afterward becomes a serious violation of human rights and dignity."

Dr. Jones closed her eyes. "You found Jesus. I cannot argue with that."

She was right. I had found Jesus. In a sense, I had known him all my life. Or, rather, I knew a lot *about* him, but my personal understanding of him was truncated, flat. In Medjugorje, I met Christ and his mother in a remarkable, unexplainable, vivid spiritual experience that changed my life forever. His love and mercy had washed over me. It was visceral, palpable. I felt it. It was real. But it was only the beginning. He commanded me to follow him and walk in his ways, to serve the least of his children, and to be the excellent doctor he had created me to be. Now it was up to me to respond with obedience and perseverance toward wherever he led me.

Dr. Jones said that she understood my perspective but disagreed with my conclusion. She didn't like abortions and how commonplace they had become but said it wasn't practical to be against them in all circumstances in our line of work.

"It's not just abortions, though, Dr. Jones." I took a deep breath before explaining myself. "We're creating life in the halls of this institution every day, but what about the embryos we create and then don't implant? Or what about when we implant six or seven or even nine embryos hoping to see one survive inside the womb, but when we see that five remaining embryos are thriving, we remove the four and keep the one? It isn't just abortion that I can't be a part of anymore. I've been part of creating life, but I've prevented it and destroyed it just as much, if not more. I want to cooperate with God's design for women's bodies. I have to follow him in that."

I explained to her why I was going to step away from any involvement in IVF, artificial birth control, and sterilization, as well as abortion and follow Catholic teachings on these issues. I knew she would be frustrated to hear this, since she and her husband had spent much of their career engaging pro-life advocates on the importance of IVF, but she responded with acceptance—and some trepidation.

"Thank you, John. I understand and respect your decision. But since this is a religious and private matter between you and God, please do not speak about this to the rest of the residents." She suggested she didn't want the news to spread because it might cause a "domino effect" and encourage other residents to reconsider their stances on these practices as well.

I believed God would strengthen me and any one of his children who chose to follow in his ways, and I wanted to tell her that. But I didn't. Instead, I just thanked her for her time and understanding.

Next, I spoke with the residency director who cared deeply about my success and the success of all her residents. She was an outstanding clinician and scientist and the mother of two daughters. Like Dr. Georgeanna, she also taught me a great deal about the humble art of listening to and caring for female patients. Surprisingly, her response was more encouraging than Dr. Georgeanna's. "I'm happy for you, even though I don't understand it," she assured me after I broke the news.

My residency director commented that I seemed more content and at peace than she had ever seen me. But like Dr. Georgeanna, she suggested that the less this disrupted the other residents, the better it would be for everyone. "Just keep it quiet," she told me.

But I didn't keep it quiet. I had already told one of the residents what I planned to do. He and I had had many conversations about family, fertility, and faith. After my meetings, he eagerly asked how the conversations had gone. When I told him that I had spilled the beans to our superiors, he congratulated me and told me he had been praying for me. And news spread from there.

It wasn't long before my colleagues knew that I had abruptly quit all abortions. Some of the attending doctors were surprised when I stepped in to help their patients suffering from damage done to their uterus or cervix during an abortion, but no one confronted me about my change of heart.

While I was grateful that my decision didn't seem to create much conflict among my colleagues, coming out as the pro-life Catholic resident wasn't all easy. The battle was

internal. I had two and a half years left of my residency to
work side by side with other doctors and residents whom
I respected but with whom I probably disagreed. It was a
constant fight to fix my gaze on Christ and follow where I
felt the Lord was leading me.

I reminded myself that I was operating from the conviction that an unborn human being is a human child, the
"second patient" in all that I did as an OB/GYN. That
reality is affirmed by science—genetics tells us that the
human embryo is a human being, and embryology and
cell biology tell us this human being is alive. If human
life begins at conception, the very moment of fertilization, then anything we do that deliberately threatens its
development or destroys it is immoral. In the OB/GYN
world, where life begins when we say it does, the pro-
life position is considered antiwoman and backward—
such a stance is a career killer. But, my experiences in
Medjugorje and Mexico City were so real, so gripping,
that I could not deny them. I strove to walk step by
step in faith, providing excellent medicine to the patients
before me.

Quitting abortions was the obvious first step for me
to take, but the conviction that life begins when egg and
sperm join—when two become one flesh—has other
implications for the physician and the Christian. One of
the hardest decisions for me was to walk away from in
vitro fertilization as well.

Infertility is complex to treat, because it is often accompanied by deep-seated shame, guilt, and anger. Seeing
patients suffer through it broke my heart, which is why
I had found the work of IVF under Dr. Georgeanna so
satisfying. I was thrilled to have the opportunity to co-
create life alongside God for women who had struggled to
conceive naturally.

However, IVF embryos were considered valuable only if they were wanted by the parents. By disposing of defective or "extra" embryos on a frequent basis, we weren't respecting human life. We were manipulating it. We were using it to obtain the highest birth-per-transfer procedure rate to show our prowess and expertise at the Jones Institute. This wasn't unconditional love for a child, a unique member of our human family. I had to admit that disposing of IVF embryos instead of implanting them is no different from abortion.

In a typical treatment prescribed by the attending physicians at the Jones Institute, 20 or more eggs might be retrieved and fertilized to conceive embryos. Of those fertilized embryos, up to 4 would be placed in the woman's uterus. At other IVF centers in the United States at that time, 9 or more embryos would be placed in the uterus. These were the Wild West days of in vitro. The rate of multiples was astronomical and dangerous for both fetus and mother. Miscarriages were common, and the wastage rate of embryos was high.

I was working in the early days of this new technology, and we were having great success in the field. But by the nature of the process, human life was being destroyed at a far higher rate than even in the abortion side of the business. While embryo wastage rates have improved with time and technology, human life is still often sacrificed during the IVF process today. Is it ethical to sacrifice innocent children so that scientists can deliver one child to a desperate family? Is it ever right to use a human being as a thing, as a product to be made and destroyed at will? Though these are difficult questions, I came to the conclusion that the answer to both of them is no.

In addition to the disposal of human embryos, there is another moral problem with IVF. As a wise doctor told me, contraception is making love while trying not to make a child; in vitro fertilization is making a child without making love; and abortion is the unmaking of a child. In each case, the dignity of the child is being denied. It is denied with IVF because the process makes the child a product, a thing, that can be used or thrown away at will instead of a person to be loved.

My decision to go all in on life-affirming medicine also meant giving up direct sterilization, which mutes the gift of fertility. I would no longer perform or supervise younger residents performing tubal ligations ("tube tying"), and I stopped signing off on them as the senior resident. Rather than disfiguring a woman's body, against God's design, in order to cut off the possibility of life, my new emphasis was on cooperating with the language of her body in order to achieve or to avoid pregnancy. The way I saw it, women were sacrificing their bodily integrity, their physiology, to preclude the possibility of life—sometimes because their partners either did not want to discuss the deeper commitment issues or just wanted to leave the responsibility for reproduction all up to the woman.

Beyond sterilization, I also came to see that birth control pills and IUDs are a harmful interruption of the gift of fertility—the gift that allows us to cooperate with God, to bring new life to earth, and to enlarge the human family. Hormonal and instrumental manipulation comes with potential negative side effects. In the 1960s, the high estrogen component of contraceptives was needed to prevent ovulation, but it also presented a risk for heart attacks and strokes. By the time I was in residency, the second- and third-generation progestins and the lowered estrogen doses were being introduced in different pills at different strengths and durations to minimize the side effects and maximize the prevention of fertilization. But these newer oral contraceptives still altered blood-clotting mechanisms and elevated the risk of blood clots and other side effects, including abnormal bleeding, headaches, weight gain, and depression. I found that many of my patients were open to the natural cooperative means of avoiding or achieving pregnancy, even if only to dodge these side effects.

It is also important to understand that many artificial birth control methods prevent an embryo from implanting in the uterus. Birth control pills and IUDs can end the life of a unique human being. However rare, this abortifacient effect was a risk I was no longer willing to take. Rather, I came to believe, I needed to help my patients respect themselves as women by choosing family planning methods that cooperated with their bodies instead of polluting them (and the environment, by the way) with harmful substances.

God helped me see a more beautiful vision for fertility and childbearing. Love is accepting God's plan, following Jesus and whatever he tells you, despite the sacrifice, and that is where happiness and joy are to be found. Fertility is a biological reality and not an ailment to be cured. Children are to be welcomed as gifts of God and not seen as an unwanted side effect of intercourse, like a sexually transmitted disease. Husbands and wives can sacrifice their bodies and feelings for the good of the other, in love, offering each other the gift of their entire selves. This self-giving then spills over into the love they offer their children, who are not looked upon as "mistakes" or commodities. This is the revelation of God in Scripture, which begins with Genesis, where God creates man and woman in his image and joins them in marriage to become one flesh, and ends with the wedding feast of the Lamb in Revelation. Obstetrics and gynecology should be in the service of God's gifts of creation and marriage.

God changed my mindset from one of believing I needed to control many aspects of conception and birth to one of being cooperative, open to his grace and providence, and seeing children as the priceless gifts that they are. Of course, I was not blind to the daily suffering of patients dealing with miscarriage, stillbirth, infertility, or disease. In fact, not only did I view the gift of life differently, I began to view the suffering differently as well. I began to see suffering not as a punishment or an unfortunate reality merely to be avoided, but as an opportunity to trust God's plan more than our human understanding. Suffering is never for nothing, and I fought hard to remember that truth as I delivered disappointing test results to my patients, grieving with them in the tender knowledge that "the LORD is near to the brokenhearted" (Ps 34:18).

Abandoning these mainstream medical practices—abortion, IVF, contraception, and sterilization—at first felt like scientifically disarming myself as a doctor. I didn't have all the weapons to fight off suffering and "rescue" my patients from their troubles, as I thought I had done in the past. Science provided physiological information and medical interventions, but not the guidance for how to use them. Faith provided access to the deeper meaning and purpose of the body as God's creation, which led me to natural, respectful methods to achieve, space, or avoid pregnancy: fertility awareness–based methods that cooperated with God's natural design rather than suppressing it. They'd been there all along, but I'd overlooked them as serious options in my excitement to join some of my heroes in the field.

I felt a strong desire to share my decision quietly with other residents who I knew were also struggling with the requirement to perform abortions on sick children on the basis of "incompatibility with life". When they heard that

I had spoken to the resident director and Dr. Georgeanna Jones and that both had disagreed but respected my decision to refrain from these mainstream practices, they wanted to know more.

The conversations would start with the residents trying to understand what had happened to me on my trip to Medjugorje with my mother. I told them of the religious experiences that brought to light my hesitations about the soundness of what I was doing to women and their unborn children. I described the change in my attitude toward the unborn children we cared for—or at times did not care for, depending on the mothers' wishes. Life should not be valued only when it is wanted, I would explain. Human life has value and dignity because we are made in the image and likeness of God, loved by him, and redeemed by his sacrifice on the cross. Something so precious, so intrinsically valuable, deserves our highest respect and the best possible treatment.

Some of my colleagues were fellow believers who were simply trying to get through residency so that they could practice for themselves according to their own convictions. They were feeling the same awkwardness about being treated as medical vending machines, at the mercy of whatever the patient desired for her pregnancy. Their faith and their discernment of Scripture were leading them to respect all of God's creation and to treat their two patients—both mother and child—with equal dignity and care.

By graduation, several other residents had chosen not to assist with the terminations of sick babies in the womb. They, too, were feeling the incredible privilege of our station, caring for unborn children rather than ending their lives because they have Down syndrome or other conditions. God had gone before me and ministered to the hearts he'd already been preparing long before those conversations. I was simply taking him at his word, trusting the promises he'd given me through the Bible and those personal spiritual experiences in Medjugorje and Mexico City. The words of Paul to Timothy urged me to press on: "For God did not give us a spirit of [fear] but a spirit of power and love and self-control" (2 Tim 1:7). I would continue to take steps of faith, walking boldly in obedience, not fearful of what others—even my mentors and colleagues—would think.

I finished my residency with the support of most of my resident colleagues and the respect of many of my professors. I was even selected to serve as administrative chief resident my senior year, the liaison between the residents and the attending physicians, a position of leadership. One of my fellow residents gave me a parting gift, a physician's prayer stitched on a needlepoint canvas that hangs framed in my exam room today.

> O Lord, in your wisdom and power and love, you heal the sick when all other help has failed and restore men to life after life itself is done. I pray that you will light my mind with thorough knowledge of remedies for my patients' ills and touch my heart with deep compassion for their sufferings. When I stretch out my hand to minister to the sick, let me heal them with a portion of your wisdom and power. And when they are not to be healed, let me help them to a deeper faith and resignation in your love. Amen.

The Saturday after I graduated from residency, I married the love of my life, Carolyn. We had met in the hospital during one of my second-year electives while I was performing a C-section. I was notorious among my fellow residents for tying medical peri-pads to my head because I sweat profusely under the surgical lights. That day I had forgotten my makeshift headband, so I asked the nurses for a wipe. Carolyn, one of the new nurses on staff, stepped forward to wipe the sweat from my brow as they do on medical drama shows. I was immediately smitten by her and her breathtaking green eyes. She was lovely and funny, and we became friends and fell in love after I found Christ.

To this day, Carolyn figuratively wipes the sweat from my brow in countless ways. I'm convinced she has more love for Jesus in her pinky finger than I do in my whole body. Without Carolyn—the woman chosen for me by God from the beginning of time, the love of my life, the person I share everything with, my muse, my center, my heart, my vision of faith and living dangerously—I am nothing. I would not be able to live my life fully without her. She reminds me that Romans 8:28 is real, that God is working all things together for good for those who love him. But this love story deserves a book or a poem of its own. Suffice it to say, without Carolyn, I would still be a lukewarm man.

Jumping off the Cliff

1991

After returning from my honeymoon with Carolyn, I was thrilled to start our life together and begin practicing as a fully trained OB/GYN. The Lord had filled my heart with even more energy and passion for the work to which he had called me and for which, I realized, I had spent a lifetime preparing. Together with Carolyn, I was up for the challenge of living out my convictions at work, but I knew it wasn't all going to be smooth sailing. Taking up crosses and following Jesus is a daunting challenge and a profound reality of new life in Christ.

My enthusiasm to enter the field was met with a lucrative offer for an OB/GYN position that paid $200,000 a year. While the salary was tempting, I turned it down to join a pro-life practice in Maryland for a quarter of that amount. Unfortunately, working for a practice that doesn't perform abortions often means a substantive pay cut, and that was a difficult pill to swallow with all the medical school debt I was working to pay off. But I knew that accepting this salary was what I had to do to obey God, serve others, and provide the care my patients deserved.

At the Maryland practice, I worked alongside two other Christian doctors, including my good friend Paul

McCauley. They understood my medical and faith perspective and let me practice according to my conscience. I was proud of my place of work, but there were two aspects about the practice that didn't align with the type of medicine I knew I was supposed to be practicing. First, they didn't see uninsured patients who needed care but didn't have the means to pay for it. They also did not accept Medicaid, because their practice was already working on slim margins, and Medicaid paid only a fraction of the cost of the services they covered.

From a business perspective, I understood why my practice did not see the poor. Losing money is not exactly a sustainable business model. But I couldn't stop thinking back to the moment Mary and Jesus told me specifically on the hill in Medjugorje that I needed to see the underserved. I knew the word "poor" can refer to many aspects of the human condition. We can be spiritually poor by refusing to walk with God, emotionally poor by not experiencing peace and joy in our lives, physically poor because of illness or disease, materially poor by lacking financial means, and so on. I was convinced God would send me all types of patients in need on his timetable, as he saw fit, but I was puzzled as to how I would see financially needy patients.

I confided in Carolyn about some of the issues I had with my place of work. "Two becoming one flesh" has real implications for how God works. One day she asked me point-blank, "Why are you still at this practice?"

I knew what I had to do. I had to start my own OB/GYN practice that accepted the least of my sisters and brothers. I envisioned a practice that would cooperate with a woman's body to avoid or achieve pregnancy without the use of abortion, contraception, sterilization, or in vitro fertilization. But I wasn't ready just yet. I was hesitant to take such a huge step of faithful obedience. My heart was full of fear. I was afraid I would fail.

Money was my primary concern. Making ends meet when we were newlyweds had already been difficult for Carolyn and me. We were just scraping by with my salary because we were still paying off loans from medical school. My ill and elderly parents were also living with us. It was a blessing to have them at our "home hospice center" as we called it, but their presence added to my anxiety over money. Even though I knew in my heart that God would provide for us, it wasn't easy to be the so-called bread-winner in the family while sitting in a place of financial uncertainty. I suspected God was trying to teach me something important: complete and total reliance on him and his plan.

Carolyn often reassured me in her way of bringing frank clarity to any situation. "It doesn't matter if we don't have any money!" she'd tell me.

Songs often say this, I'd think, and just as often, the singer and songwriter divorce! I didn't understand how letting go of money would work out practically.

In the midst of my wavering, God never let me forget the marching orders I had received on the rocky hilltop in Medjugorje and in Guadalupe: to be the best doctor I could be, to see the poor and to see them daily, and to follow the teachings of his Church. Even though the type of practice where I was working was a safe haven for pro-life Christian doctors, it was not completely in line with what God and had instructed me to do. Carolyn would remind me of this reality. "If Jesus told you this, and the Mother of God confirmed it, why aren't we doing it?" she'd press me.

My buddy Joe called me up one day and gave me the final push I needed to catapult my faith into action. He knew I felt called to start an OB/GYN practice dedicated to total pro-woman, life-affirming medicine, what I call "merciful medicine". To me, merciful medicine meant caring for *two* patients, mother and child, as full human beings in every sense—physical and spiritual. It meant respecting female fertility, treating children with compassion at each moment of biological growth, grieving alongside mothers and fathers when a pregnancy is lost, and welcoming all patients in need—regardless of their financial situation. Joe confronted me about why I hadn't started moving forward on this vision. "What are you doing, John? God is talking to you and you're not listening. That's disobedience!" Everyone needs an honest friend like Joe, willing to speak the truth even if it stings a little. He encouraged me, too. "God doesn't need you, but he loves you. Just listen to him and don't worry about the details."

Joe's words pierced my heart. I needed to take courage, get over my fears, and jump into Christ's side and his mother's arms—under his mercy and her mantle. It was time to start a new kind of practice, one that offered all women Christ-centered health care, whether or not they had financial means and whether or not they were abortion-minded. I had delayed long enough. I just needed some seed funds to get started.

The next day, I broke the news to Dr. McCauley that I would be leaving his practice, after over two years, to start a pro-life, faith-based obstetrics and gynecology practice for all women—insured, uninsured, and underinsured. He said he understood and wished me luck, and we remain close friends.

Unfortunately, money continued to be a challenge. But I reminded myself that Jesus is never outdone in generosity. With only $5,000 of seed money that a friend donated to us and a lot of faith, my wife and I started Tepeyac Family

Center. Carolyn served as the nurse and office manager, and I was the only doctor. We were both the cleaning crew, and eventually our boys were the entertainment for the children who came with their mothers.

I named the medical practice after Tepeyac Hill in Mexico so that I would never forget the moment in the cathedral when the divine voice asked me, "Why are you hurting me?" I kept the name Tepeyac despite some negative feedback I received: that it was difficult to pronounce and might not be a good choice from a marketing perspective. But it's there, still, to remind me that the work I am called to is far deeper than medical metrics, lab results, and cookbook approaches to medicine. Obstetrics and gynecology is a matter of life, death, love, marriage, and family.

My heart had been hard for a long time. Fear had been my operating emotion, and procrastination waiting on perfection my modus operandi. But through a merciful Savior's love, Tepeyac opened its doors in February 1994. We set out with a bold mission: to restore health and integrity to the human person by combining the best of modern medicine with the healing presence of Jesus Christ.

Carolyn and my friend Bob, who gave us the seed money, urged me to start seeing patients even though we couldn't afford an office yet. And so Carolyn and I saw patients in our northern Virginia home, on our living room couch covered with plastic and paper. Our only form of advertising was word of mouth from past and current patients, local pregnancy centers, fertility awareness practitioners, and churches with which we were connected. We offered home births and obtained admitting privileges at a nearby hospital for hospital births and surgeries.

By May, two friends of mine, Dr. Joe Evers and Dr. Bill McCarthy, allowed me to spend one day a week in each of their offices for minimal rent. By October, we had a steady flow of patients and had accrued enough cash to rent an office suite. In that first year, I delivered 45 babies.

A few months into our first year in practice, Bob, our initial investor, persuaded his pro-life priest friends to invest in us so that we could rent an office full-time. I promised I would pay them back within three years with interest higher than any bank would give them. They and several families lent us $65,000, which we paid back with interest in one year.

However, the financial challenge of seeing uninsured and underinsured patients persisted. Carolyn and I were committed to never turning away a woman in need. We eventually gained the resources to hire more staff, and every time one of our accountants warned me we had to cut back on how many poor or uninsured patients we were covering, I would remind him that making money had never been our primary objective. That's something accountants don't usually like to hear. Our ultimate goal was to share Christ's love in the form of merciful medicine, whether or not that industry was a big money-making enterprise.

My reasoning was that my job as a doctor is to love God and neighbor in my daily work. But what does this look like practically? How do you *really* love God with all your heart, soul, strength, and mind while also loving your neighbor as yourself as an OB/GYN?

For me, loving God and neighbor as a doctor means seeing everyone who walks in the door—the wealthy, the needy, the spiritually impoverished, the spiritually rich—and offering to all excellent medicine that is aligned with God's truth.

Jesus himself said, "As you did it to one of the least of these my brethren, you did it to me" (Mt 25:40). Did I know what the cash flow was going to be during the first few years? No. But from those first months to today, God has sent me rich, poor, sick, and healthy patients, and we have seen the vast majority of them. God has remained faithful in providing for us. We have always had just what we needed to get by from month to month. He has taught me to trust in the value of sacrifice and the profound power of almsgiving.

Tepeyac transitioned to a nonprofit nine years after its inception in order to raise more money for the uninsured and underinsured patients. This was how we married "business" with our seemingly upside-down business model. With that change, we were able to provide financial assistance to the 25 to 35 percent of our pregnant patients who were on Medicaid, being charged on a sliding scale, or being seen through partnerships with pregnancy centers. I kept repeating the message I believe Mary delivered to me in Medjugorje: the key is to see the poor, and all else will follow.

We didn't want only to see the financially needy at Tepeyac; we also wanted to minister to the spiritual needs of our patients. We were in one of the richest areas in America: Fairfax County, Virginia. While there were plenty of women in need of financial assistance, spiritual poverty is everywhere. I am all too familiar with it myself.

Carolyn pushed me through financial challenges and cared for me through illnesses that distracted me and threatened my ability to work. I fought metastatic testicular cancer, a coma, a broken neck, pancreatitis, morbid obesity, and diabetes—all in the early years of Tepeyac while we were getting it off the ground.

Interestingly enough, the type of cancerous tumor I had would have given me a positive pregnancy test. It produces the hormone hGC, the same hormone that a developing placenta produces in a woman's uterus. Oncologists found cancerous lymph nodes along my spine and up to my head. I would require surgery and chemotherapy. I also experienced extreme nausea and vomiting from the cancer and chemo—what I imagine severe morning sickness must be like for my patients. Talk about the Lord touching "my heart with deep compassion for their sufferings", as the needlepoint in my physician's prayer reads. God taught me by making me the patient.

While I was recovering from cancer, I often wondered why God would call me to start a medical practice only to pull me away. But even in my absence, God showed me he was at work. He used my suffering and the time away from my patients to show me that, like financial hardship, physical hardship is a great opportunity to learn to trust in him.

I'll never forget when a priest told me in confession that God would work without me. Wow. That was the Lord stripping my pride. I was at the service of the Savior and Creator of the world, and he knew what was best for me. His grace was sufficient in my weakness. Ultimately, he used my agony to unleash joy by showing me that he would always provide.

The Lord also showed me Carolyn's unwavering love for me as she stood by my side and took care of me when I was sick. When I procrastinated on paperwork out of fatigue or became fearful that Tepeyac would fall apart while I was getting chemo, Carolyn would always remind me that everything I had done in my life, both good and bad, had been a preparation for now. "Johnny, you have to do whatever he tells you," she would say. "Don't you ever deny Jesus and Mary."

By that she meant that no matter the challenges we were facing, we needed to trust God always. In moments of exhaustion and doubt, my confidence in God would falter, but Carolyn kept me walking in obedience with the Lord day by day even when I felt the weight of a million stresses. Her faith was stronger than mine.

God gave me the grace to get through suffering, not around it. He taught me what real love is by redeeming my life and accompanying me through every step of his plan.

We were running a specialty practice in a world where medicine is largely about manipulating human bodies for money. Patients are sometimes treated as mere consumers. In many areas, technology has replaced touch and face-to-face interaction. Numerical risk-benefit calculations have nearly eclipsed ethical considerations. Abortion is considered reproductive health care. In short, the relationship between patient and doctor has become brief and commercialized.

It's incredible where human ingenuity has taken modern medicine: the length and quality of life has been extended for many people. But are the latest developments in medicine always or necessarily better than the older methods of care? When I opened my practice, many new medicines and treatments were then, and still are today, driven by corporate profits with minimal improvements in health outcomes. I had to be discerning about whatever was new and popular in obstetrics and gynecology and choose only those interventions that respected human dignity.

I'd often say that the missing vitamin in a lot of medical care is vitamin R for "relationship". At Tepeyac, we wanted to strengthen the relationships between doctor and patient, mother and child, wife and husband, and family and community. Repairing earthly relationships points us back to Christ, who mends the relationship between us and God and asks us to let him help us to mend our relationships with each other. It's my job as a doctor to understand the many factors that play a role in the health of my patients, including their relationships.

I believe many health conditions can have better outcomes when a patient is surrounded by a loving family and community and when medical professionals are willing to do the relational work alongside the medical than when a patient receives only medical attention. Excellent women's health care requires listening, collaborating, and cooperatively treating patients as people within a network of relationships, not as solitary consumers. Both physical and spiritual health flourish within sacrificial relationships between patients and their families, patients and their doctors, and patients and God.

Like housing the homeless, clothing the naked, and feeding the hungry, caring for the sick is an act of mercy. At least, it should be. At Tepeyac we try to offer *merciful medicine*. That means we treat two patients, mother and child. We care for each one as a whole individual with a body and an eternal soul.

Every woman, whether rich or poor in whatever material or spiritual sense, deserves merciful medicine. All women deserve a gynecologist who does not laugh at them when they say they are abstinent or not using contraceptives. They deserve an obstetrician who affirms that their loss after a miscarriage is the real loss of a child, supports their decision to carry their sick child to term, and does not ask if they'd like to have their tubes tied immediately after their second child is born. They deserve a medical practice that serves every woman, regardless of financial situation, and cares for their unborn baby at every stage of biological development.

Sometimes we have to make tough choices, such as choosing whether or not to put a terminally ill newborn on life support and, if so, for how long. But discerning how long to prolong life artificially is far different from directly intervening to end life unnaturally. We have to abandon the idea that killing babies who are sick or less than "perfect" is somehow merciful. The physician's job is to attempt to relieve pain and suffering and, when unable to do so, to give it up to our Father, the Great Physician. It is never to kill. We are to love even the sickest children just for who they are, despite any illness or defect.

At Tepeyac, we call this love for the sickest babies "perinatal hospice". We treat the womb as a hospice center that provides the parents time to be with their baby as it dies a natural death rather than abort the child. Along with the parents, we love that baby until the end of his earthly life. This approach to babies who are diagnosed with a life-limiting disease or birth defect reminds us that every life, no matter how short, has value. Every human person deserves to be honored as a member of our family, whether he is a young embryo, an unborn child with Down syndrome, or a little baby who has passed away in the womb.

If patients have had abortions in the past, no matter the reason, we meet them with compassion and understanding. We offer prayer and post-abortion healing resources where appropriate. Jesus teaches us to condemn the sin, not the sinner. We strive to emulate him in all that we do, especially when we care for women who have suffered the pain and trauma of abortion.

A woman who has had an abortion is changed forever, whether she knows it or not. These women are often deeply wounded. Some experience depression, guilt and regret, rage and anger, nightmares, intense grief, or suicidal thoughts. Others seem unchanged or apathetic on the outside, but I have found that most feel as though the abortion experience has left a hole in their heart. Some may wrongly believe they don't deserve to be loved or forgiven after having aborted their children, and they let these beliefs destroy them from the inside out. They often experience a crisis with a future pregnancy, especially if it ends in a miscarriage or stillbirth. Occasionally, these women feel guilty when they deliver a healthy baby, believing they don't deserve another child because of the one they rejected.

I remind my post-abortive patients that love, forgiveness, and hope always lie on the other side of sin and sorrow—I would know. I cannot cast any stones, because I am no better. I do my best to meet these women where they are and listen to them, allowing them to unburden themselves. I often refer them for continued counseling or to a post-abortion healing program called Project Rachel to further their emotional and spiritual healing.

Tepeyac is also dedicated to respecting God's design for the body by offering holistic gynecology and adolescent care. We teach teens the beauty of obedient abstinence, not by sending a message of fear about pregnancy or showing them graphic images of sexually transmitted diseases, but by sharing a message of love and virtue that holds up sex as beautiful and sacred within the context of marriage. When teens do get pregnant, we meet them with compassion and help them navigate their concerns and fears. We affirm them in their dignity as temples of the Holy Spirit and encourage them to prioritize their emotional, physical, and spiritual health.

Now, I am well aware that there are different opinions among believers on some of these topics, particularly on birth control and sterilization. I serve and love patients with different convictions regarding family planning and have many faithful, Christ-following friends with opinions

different from my own. But it is my conviction that the
Gospel is at the core of the reason that we shouldn't re-
engineer our bodies by muting fertility. Jesus became a
man with a physical body, and that means something.
Bodies matter. God sanctifies our bodies as temples of
the Holy Spirit. Destroying procreative powers alters the
physical body, our temples, against his design. Our bodies
are to be loved and respected as God has created them, not
abused and disfigured.

Birth control methods such as the pill and IUDs can
harm the body through hormonal interference. They
mute fertility and have the potential to increase a woman's risk of breast cancer,[1] blood clots, strokes, heart
attacks, and in rare cases, death.[2] These methods also
have the potential to abort young embryos that would
otherwise successfully implant, due to the thin uterine
lining caused by the excess progesterone from the pill or
IUD. Not only can contraceptives be potentially harmful
to the woman's body and the unborn, they can closes
our bodies off to our spouses and our hearts off to God's
gift of life.

Nearly the same can be said for direct female sterilization, when ovarian tubes are permanently closed, cut, or
removed. "Tube tying" is a permanent decision that dis-
figures the natural, healthy function of a woman's reproductive biology and shuts down the possibility of life.
What might saying no to God's biological design reveal
about our trust in him and his gift of life? Sterilization and

[1] "Birth Control Pills", Susan G. Komen (website), last modified February 24, 2021, https://www.komen.org/breast-cancer/risk-factor/birth-control
-pills/#:~:text=Current%20or%20recent%20use%20of,36%2C38%2D39%5D.

[2] Lynn Keenan and Gerard Migeon, "Birth Control, Blood Clots, and
Untimely Death: Time to Reconsider What We Tell Our Teens?", *Public Dis-
course*, March 4, 2019, https://www.thepublicdiscourse.com/2019/03/49896/.

birth control are not just medical issues, but deeply spiritual ones.

Fertility is a gift to support, not a disease to be repressed. And God has given us the ability to be good stewards of our fertility and to plan pregnancies by listening to the incredible language of a woman's body. At Tepeyac, we teach fertility awareness methods that allow women to identify the fertile windows of their cycles. These methods are healthy and holistic and cooperate with the gift of a woman's fertility instead of disabling it.

Current fertility awareness methods are not like the inaccurate calendar-counting-only methods of the past. Since then, doctors and scientists have been able to give women the tools to listen to the "language of their body". Signs such as cervical mucus, body temperature, and cycle patterns offer a deeper understanding of a woman's fertility. New technology including hormone-change monitors, ovulation test strips, and cycle-tracking apps have made fertility awareness easier than ever.

Fertility awareness honors the body, while contraceptive technologies can harm, impede, silence, and tamper with it. Today, fertility awareness methods are 99 percent effective[3] when practiced correctly, which is more effective than condoms (98 percent) and just as effective as birth control pills and IUDs. These women-empowering approaches have given my patients a better understanding of their bodies and more control in managing their fertility.

When it comes to infertility, our goal at Tepeyac is to restore the body back to God's design rather than turn to

[3] "Natural Family Planning (Fertility Awareness)—Your Contraception Guide", NHS (website of the National Health Service of England), last reviewed April 13, 2021, https://www.nhs.uk/conditions/contraception/natural-family-planning/.

methods like IVF that create human embryos as if they were products manufactured for consumption and then implant, freeze, or discard them at will. Instead, we use Natural Procreative Technology (NaPro Technology), which is a method for identifying and treating the root cause of infertility. By closely charting a woman's menstrual cycle, we can identify health problems, including endometriosis, ovarian cysts, polycystic ovarian syndrome, and hormonal abnormalities. Rather than using IVF to bypass the disease that causes childlessness, we attack endometriosis with surgery, open ovarian tubes, and augment hormones of the endocrine system to maximize fertility without resorting to procedures that manufacture embryos. We can even treat some causes of infertility with nutrition, herbs, and vitamins.

Sometimes we can find no medical explanation or cure for infertility. Many women feel like their bodies are broken and wonder why God has given them the desire to be a mother without the ability to fulfill that desire naturally. And that's exactly it—infertility often reveals the good and natural desire of a woman's heart. For that reason, doctors must treat the whole woman, body and soul. We offer to pray with our patients who are aching to conceive and recommend infertility support groups. I often assure my patients, "If Christ is the Lord of your life, you better believe he is also the Lord of your fertility."

I've been blessed to witness many patients transformed by the healing power of Jesus Christ and merciful medicine. They are daily reminders that there is a life of abundant joy to be found when we abandon the "my body, my choice" mantra and replace it with "my body given up for you". Christ's ultimate display of love for us on the cross beckons every mother to follow his example of loving sacrifice with the stretching and scarring of her body as she brings forth new life.

I often think about a picture that my good friend Dr. Marie Anderson hung in her office at Tepeyac OB/GYN. The photograph shows her standing at the edge of a high diving cliff over a cove in the Pacific Ocean as she hesitates before she jumps. She joined Tepeyac six weeks later and kept that picture in her office to remind her that trusting God can sometimes be like jumping off a cliff—totally terrifying.

Marie joined our practice in 1997, and, like me, she had experienced a renewal of her faith while in medical residency where she saw discrepancies between Church teaching and standard OB/GYN practice. Leaving her former practice to join Tepeyac felt like taking a trust fall off a giant cliff into God's arms and believing he would be there to catch her.

I understood that feeling completely. It can be stomach-in-your-throat nerve-racking to trust God. For the longest time, I didn't want to jump off the cliff and start Tepeyac. For years, I sat contently in my lukewarm faith. I cared more about the approval of my professors and colleagues than the approval of God. Even when he brought me back to him, I still doubted and feared and let my pride take over. I dragged my feet to the place I knew he was calling me. But the Great Physician healed me, a diseased sinner. He led me, through the persistent help of my wife, Carolyn, to abandon a comfortable life in order to build a culture of life through Tepeyac.

From the beginning, God has guided and protected Tepeyac OB/GYN and helped us to further its work. He assured me that he would take care of everything else when I put him first and trusted him. Eventually, I said yes to God, and the anxiety of jumping off the cliff was

replaced with joy and a peace that transcends all understanding. But as Dr. Marie Anderson would often remind
me in reference to her photograph, "Jumping is only the
beginning."

12

Go Forth

I held the hand of my three-year-old son, John Paul, leading him quickly toward a small chapel on the outskirts of
Washington, D.C., as the first rays of morning stretched
across the sky. With us were my parents and Carolyn, car-
rying our new baby, Joseph, bundled up and still asleep in
her arms.

If there was a day to get to church early, today was the
day. Mother Teresa was rumored to be the guest of honor
at the six o'clock Mass at the Missionaries of Charity Con-
vent. We were determined to meet her or at least to get a
glimpse of this living saint.

I admired Mother Teresa's confidence in the power of
Jesus, her trust in God's love and mercy, and the great
compassion with which she served the poor. She lived
among them. She held them. She brought the love of
Jesus to the sick and lonely and dying. Reading about her
work in the slums of India had motivated me to serve in
Appalachia years earlier and ultimately given me courage
to try never to turn away a patient in need, even when it
didn't make sense for my practice financially. But I never
imagined I'd have the opportunity to meet this woman of
God face to face.

About 20 people stood in the hallway outside the first-floor room converted into a chapel. A fresh energy buzzed quietly through their huddle this morning. These normal-looking folks were quite invigorated for such an early hour, as they prepared to meet Jesus in the Eucharist and also possibly the woman who had followed Jesus into the slums of Calcutta. She inspired tireless, joyful service to the poor in the nation's capital and in hundreds of thousands of people around the globe.

We were asked to remove our shoes at the door, as was customary before entering a home or a place of worship in India. Some sisters in their blue-striped white saris and their visiting families waited inside on folding chairs. Some knelt in prayer. All were recollected in silence and reverence.

I studied each of the sisters' faces, but recognized none as the famous missionary from Calcutta. As I scanned the crowd, two words printed in bold black lettering on the chapel wall captured my attention: "I THIRST." The words were printed next to a crucifix, just below Christ's right arm. This short sentence was spoken by Jesus while he was on the cross just moments before his death, just after he entrusted Mary to his beloved disciple, John, as recorded in John's Gospel (19:28). My heart marveled at this short statement, coming from the cross just before he gave up his life for me. How could the one who calls himself the Source of Living Water have any thirst? Yet, he thirsted, and he wanted us to know that.

What could Christ have possibly thirsted for in his final moments? In just two words, he highlighted his humanity, fulfilled prophecy (Ps 69:21), and pointed to a reality deeper than words can describe. Jesus thirsted for more than water. But for what? What could God possibly desire? My mind failed to wrap itself around the significance of Christ's yearning. *What does this truly mean, Lord?*, my heart wondered while we waited for Mass to begin. *What do you thirst for, Lord? How do you want us to respond to your thirst? Do I thirst in this way?* I had hoped for a divine response or even a fragment of Scripture I could mull over, but none came to me.

At the end of the Mass, the sisters began folding up the chairs and moved to the right side of the room to make a path for their guests. Still, there was no sign of Mother Teresa. Disheartened and a bit confused, we began making our way toward the exit.

Just then, one of the sisters asked us to line up along the left side of the chapel wall. My heart leapt with a flash of hope as we took our place. We couldn't see her yet, but I sensed she was there, speaking softly to the family at the front of the line.

Just a few moments later, the group in front of us turned to leave. Their exit revealed a tiny woman standing in front of me. Dark, deep-set eyes gazed peacefully out from underneath the blue border of her sari. Her face was aged with wisdom and radiant with joy. Her hands clasped gently in front of her diminutive and hunched frame. It was no wonder we had not spotted her earlier. She was so little, so unassuming, and so at peace.

The lines around the edges of her eyes pinched together as she reached her hands forward, first to Mom, then to Dad. Mom had never been much of a talker to strangers, but in the presence of this heroine of the faith, she became quite the babbler. Mom expressed her gratitude for her visit and asked for her prayers. Next thing I knew, she and Dad were bragging about their children, including me, to Mother Teresa. I looked away, trying to conceal my embarrassment. "I'm here with my son; he's a doctor. He runs an OB/GYN practice in Northern Virginia and he sees the underserved."

Mother Teresa nodded and smiled kindly. She seemed less interested in my accomplishments and more interested in meeting my Carolyn and our sons. She reached up and placed her palms affectionately on Carolyn's cheek. Her words traveled with a speed that matched her movements, without any hurry as if we were the only family in the world at that moment. "Bless you in the name of Jesus," she said humbly to Carolyn, giving her a Miraculous Medal, which she has to this day. She gave Miraculous Medals to nearly everyone she encountered, reminding them to pray and to stay close to Jesus, as Mary did.

Next she bent down to little John Paul and scooped him up for a big squeeze. Carolyn passed baby Joseph to her. She received him gently into her arms and rocked him back and forth, looking into his eyes and soul. The scene offered a snapshot of how I imagine Jesus interacted with little children, taking them into his arms without hesitation, welcoming them and delighting in their presence.

Then, Mother Teresa turned to me. "You're the doctor?" she asked.

"Yes, Mother," I said, trying to play it cool and hide how starstruck I truly was. I added that I delivered babies and cared for women.

Her hands enfolded mine. "Come to Calcutta and help me."

Shocked, flattered, and wondering if she was serious all at once, I paused to gather my response. *Did Mother Teresa really just ask me to join her ministry in India?* I briefly wondered if this was one of those moments God was calling me to do something crazy. I responded in the only way I knew how. "Mother, I work in one of the richest counties in America. I see patients who are poor and patients who are rich, but poor in spirit. At my clinic, we want to offer our patients more than just medicine. We want to offer them an act of mercy through the Holy Spirit." I paused, taking a deep breath. "But, if you think I should, I will go to Calcutta with you."

She stepped closer, her eyes locked on mine. "You have brought Calcutta to Virginia. Stay there and build the Kingdom."

In that moment, it was as if I were looking into the eyes of Christ. Her words, saturated with the Father's love and peace, humbled me and confirmed my calling to *merciful medicine* in America. "Stay here and do the work of Jesus. I will pray for you," she said, giving me her calling card, the Miraculous Medal.

As soon as we piled in the car for the drive back home, I hung the medal on my rearview mirror. The imprint of Mary with her arms outstretched to me twisted slowly back and forth as I started the engine. On the back of the medal is a cross with the letter *M* below it, representing Mary at the foot of the cross as she is described in John 19:25. Just three verses later, Jesus cries out in thirst.

I imagined Mary as a loving mother, racked with grief as she watched her son suffer one of the most horrific forms of capital punishment known to mankind, wanting nothing but to satiate his thirst. In that moment, in his full humanity, Jesus thirsted for water, for he had lost a great deal of blood; but on a deeper level, he was thirsting for souls to love him and their neighbors. And he provides the love for us to do this. As he tells the woman at the well, the water he gives becomes in us "a spring of water welling up to eternal life" (Jn 4:14).

Mother Teresa took Christ's thirst seriously. She responded to his need on the cross by kneeling before him in prayer—receiving and returning his love—and then kneeling at the bedsides of the sick and dying, holding their hands, sharing the Gospel with them, and cherishing them, even in their last moments on this earth. When she did these things, she did them for Jesus, just as he said (Mt 25:40). She was quenching his thirst.

Even long after those precious moments in the chapel, the significance of my encounter with Mother Teresa stays with me to this day. With such few words, she helped me to understand better Christ's thirst on the cross and how he wants me to respond. I'm not sure I would have used the same words Mother Teresa did, that I have brought Calcutta to Virginia. But her words offered me the affirmation I needed in the moment, that I was right where God wanted me, responding to Christ's thirst in the unique way he had given to me.

I hope that Tepeyac is a drop of water in a spiritually dehydrated world—even though many days at work, it's hard to believe I am capable of squeezing out even one measly drop of water for Christ. I meet with patients struggling with infertility, abnormal pregnancies, and postpartum depression, and sometimes my attempts to share encouragement fall flat. My heart crumbles when an abortion-minded mother doesn't show up for her 20-week appointment and I never see her again. Staff and funding challenges and complicated business decisions come in regular waves. Ultimately, I am powerless without Christ. I simply entrust my patients and all of our challenges to his love and mercy. Christ can turn a drop of water in a desert into an infinite pool (Ps 107:35).

We've been blessed to deliver thousands of healthy babies at Tepeyac and hire several excellent doctors and mid-level providers who are loyal to the mission and principles of our practice. We've established a "perinatal hospice program" with the help of Dr. Marie Anderson and launched an educational resource center to provide pro-life medical information to medical professionals and clergy. Our doctors have been invited to speak nationwide at churches and medical schools and even in front of Congress and the United Nations. We have helped inspire a growing network of medical practices across the country modeled on life-affirming medicine. The Holy Spirit is renewing and will continue to renew the face of medicine on earth into a culture of life. This is happening through his children who are willing to follow his lead, to be his instruments in their work, and to keep running the race with their eyes fixed on Jesus.

I continued to reflect on Christ's thirst on the cross for his people and God's provision for Tepeyac OB/GYN as we drove home past marble monuments and government office buildings. The Miraculous Medal of Mary flickered in the sunshine, reminding me of the extraordinary way God chose a young woman in Nazareth to undo the curse of Eve and give birth to our Savior. It reminded me of the unexpected way he had saved a Jersey guy with a hardened heart on a hilltop, halfway across the world. It reminded me of the love a mother has for her children. It reminded me of my *two* patients and how we are all united by heavenly grace and human genetics. We are part of *one human family*: his family.

CONCLUSION

Hope at the Improv

Recently, I spoke to students in the Future Medical Professionals for Life at the University of Virginia. They asked questions about everything from when life begins to health policy to how to achieve their professional goals. I did not have all the answers, but I urged them to enter into medicine because we need the next generation to carry on life-affirming medicine in America. I challenged them, asking, "If he calls you, are you going to obey?"

Following Christ by embracing *merciful medicine* does three things: First it helps our hearts soften to the cry of the sick and the poor as they teach us the love of Jesus. Second, through merciful medicine, we serve the least of our family members and thus serve Jesus. And third, as witnesses, we become a beacon of light and hope in our community, showing the power of the love of God to transform us and society at large. I know that pursuing a career like this may not seem practical in today's America.

For 2,000 years, the light of Christ has illuminated Western civilization. But in our own day, many people have rejected the Christian culture of life and embraced a culture of death. Using modern science and technology, they seek to be their own gods—creating, manipulating, and ending human lives at will through artificial reproduction, abortion, euthanasia, and so on. Doctors are under tremendous pressure to go along with the latest trends, even when they violate their consciences.

At times, it may feel as though our modern society is imploding in chaos around us. As my father constantly warned, countries fall from within by deviating from their principles, changing the meanings of words in their laws, and losing sight of the good, beautiful, and true. We legalize the immoral, keep silent at the violence toward the innocent, and jettison the Judeo-Christian pillars that hold up our society. But we remember that the dissonance that collapses human foundations and rattles our hearts cannot be corrected without Christ.

My conversion story could be anyone's. It's nothing special. We all have sinned, and yet God has led every one of us on unique paths, never letting us down or leaving our side. God invites all of us to be humble enough to repent and flexible enough to put away our plans and embrace the course that he places in front of us, even when it doesn't seem practical.

Following Christ may often feel like acting in an improv show: we have plans, he intervenes, and we change course. We adapt to his plan, remembering that each moment and opportunity has been allowed or willed by our Father. Our Abba. Following his plan often looks different from how we might have imagined it, but when we cooperate with the Holy Spirit, we participate in the renewal of the face of the earth. For me, that involves medicine. For you, it involves the circumstances you find yourself in. As his mother reminds us, "Do whatever he tells you" (Jn 2:5).

Difficulties are on the horizon for our society and for each of us, but we can still love the Lord during difficult times. We can still love today among the chaos and confusion. We can live our calling in the midst of religious and political persecution as heroes in history have demonstrated. Dietrich Bonhoeffer taught that grace is costly and requires sacrifice. We must rejoice in God's mercy *and* remember that "When Christ calls a man, he bids him come and die."[1] This is where real hope is found.

To know and love the true God gives hope. Those who hope in the Lord "will renew their strength" (Is 40:31). Are you disturbed within? Put your hope in God (Ps 42:11). He is our Savior, and our hope is in him, "all the day long" (Ps 25:5).

So when the time comes to sacrifice for his love, and you need to live Colossians 1:24 and rejoice in your sufferings, remember that "suffering produces endurance, and endurance produces character, and character produces hope" (Rom 5:3–4).

This is our time. We are here today, right where he has us, for a reason.

For life-affirming medical resources or to support the mission of Tepeyac OB/GYN, visit divinemercycare.org.

---

[1] Dietrich Bonhoeffer, *The Cost of Discipleship* (New York: Simon & Schuster, 1995), 89.